THE BERLIN AIRLIFT

THE BERLIN AIRLIFT

Robert Jackson, *1941-*

Patrick Stephens
Wellingborough, Northamptonshire

© Robert Jackson 1988

First published in 1988

British Library Cataloguing in Publication Data

Jackson, Robert, *1941*
    Berlin airlift.
    1. Berlin (Germany) — Blockade,
    1948–1949
    I. Title
    943'.1554'087   DD881

    ISBN 0-85059-881-8

*Patrick Stephens is part of the
Thorsons Publishing Group,
Wellingborough, Northamptonshire,
NN8 2RQ, England.*

Printed in Great Britain by Adlard and Son
Limited, The Garden City Press, Letchworth,
Hertfordshire

10 9 8 7 6 5 4 3 2 1

Contents

Acknowledgements

My primary source of information on the Berlin Airlift was the archives of the Air Historical Branch, Ministry of Defence (RAF). For access to these I am indebted to Air Commodore Henry Probert MBE MA and to his staff, in particular to Sebastian Cox BA MA who gave up a lot of his time to assist me in my researches.

As far as published works are concerned, one of the best and most entertaining is *Berlin Airlift* by Robert Rodrigo (Cassell 1960), which contains many personal accounts. Frank Donovan's *Bridge in the Sky* (Hale 1970) deals mainly with the USAF's Operation Vittles and complements Rodrigo's work, while *The Siege of Berlin* by Mark Arnold-Forster (Collins 1979) provides an excellent account of life in Berlin from the Airlift to the building of the infamous wall. *Blockade* by Eric Morris (Hamish Hamilton 1973) gives the political history of the divided city in some depth, while *Berlin Blockade — a Reminder* by Max Charles (Allan Wingate 1959) does the same thing, but in more summarized form. To gain a full understanding of what happened in post-war Europe leading up to the Berlin Crisis, there are few better works than one written by the man who was at the heart of things: *Decision in Germany* by General Lucius D. Clay (Heinemann 1950); while the desperate battle for Berlin itself in 1945 is graphically described by Earl F. Ziemke in *Battle for Berlin* (Purnell 1968). Finally, my sincere thanks to Angela Tunstall for her work of typing and editing, and for compiling the appendices to this book; to Ann Harington for providing photographs; and to Dr Bob McManners for supplying the map.

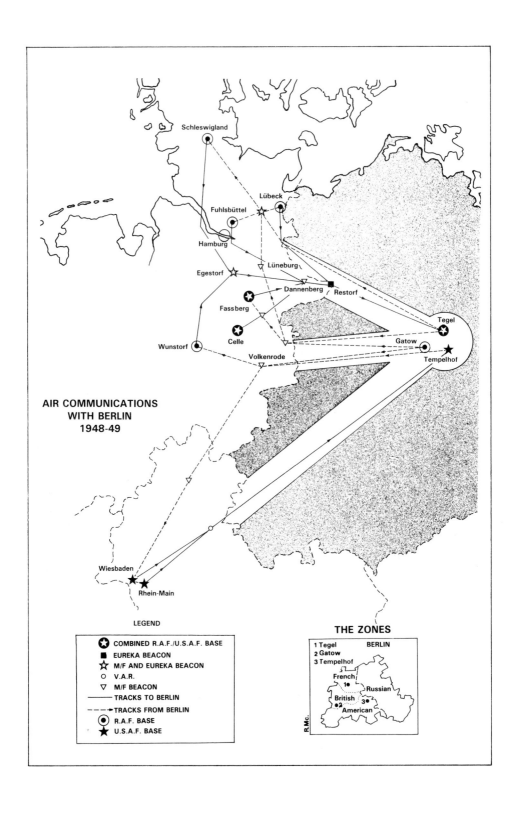

AIR COMMUNICATIONS
WITH BERLIN
1948-49

Schleswigland

Lübeck

Fuhlsbüttel

Hamburg

Lüneburg

Egestorf

Dannenberg   Restorf

Fassberg

Celle

Wunstorf

Volkenrode

Tegel

Gatow

Tempelhof

Wiesbaden

Rhein-Main

LEGEND

⊛ COMBINED R.A.F./U.S.A.F. BASE
■ EUREKA BEACON
☆ M/F AND EUREKA BEACON
○ V.A.R.
▽ M/F BEACON
—— TRACKS TO BERLIN
---→ TRACKS FROM BERLIN
⊙ R.A.F. BASE
★ U.S.A.F. BASE

THE ZONES

1 Tegel   BERLIN
2 Gatow
3 Tempelhof

French
1●
Russian
British   3●
●2
American

R.Mc.

Chapter One
An illusion of peace

At 19:22 hours local time on 23 September 1949, Douglas Dakota C Mk IV serial KN652 of No 30 Squadron, Royal Air Force, touched down on the 6,000-ft (1,829m) runway of Gatow airfield, in the British Sector of the divided city of Berlin. It had taken off from Lübeck, on the Baltic coast, 52 minutes earlier.

On the Dakota's nose there was an inscription which read: 'Positively the last load from Lübeck, 73,705 tons. Psalm 21, Verse 11.'

The first part was clear enough, but the Biblical reference was somewhat puzzling to the British servicemen and German civilians who unloaded the Dakota's cargo. Later, however, when some of the more curious among them took the trouble to look it up, they understood. Psalm 21, Verse 11, ran:

'For they intended evil against thee; they imagined a mischievous device, which they are not able to perform.'

Such, then, was the end of the story; a story that had its beginning nearly four and a half years earlier, on 1 May 1945.

At noon on that day, Guards Major Nikolai Malinovsky and Guards Captain Vladimir Novoselov, both fighter pilots with the Red Air Force's 2nd Air Army, flew low over the outskirts of Berlin in their Yakovlev Yak-3s. At 100 ft (30m) they roared along the River Spree, the broad road on its bank lined with the tanks of the 1st Guards Army. Turning over the shattered cathedral, they levelled out again and swept over the Reichstag. From their cockpits two red banners fluttered down into the hands of the Russian troops below. One carried an embroidered message of greeting: the other bore a single word — Victory.

By nightfall on 2 May, Berlin was completely occupied by Soviet forces. Adolf Hitler, the architect of Europe's misery for the best part of six years, had killed himself 48 hours earlier, and now General Weidling, commanding Berlin's defences, ordered his remaining forces to surrender.

Behind the tough and disciplined troops of the Soviet Guards Divisions who had spearheaded the assault on Berlin, and who had fought their way foot by foot through the rubble towards the centre of the city, came the support troops and reserves who were now to take their place. Their arrival heralded an orgy of rape, murder and pillage that has no parallel in the history of modern warfare. It was some time before the Russian city commandant of Berlin, Colonel-

Above left *Symbolic of the misery and despair of Hitler's Germany in the closing days of the Third Reich — a wounded Hitler Youth despatch rider, Berlin, April 1945.*

Above *Russian troops hoist the flag over the shattered Reichstag, 2 May 1945.*

Left *A Soviet T-34 tank grinds through the ruins of Berlin.*

General N.Z. Berzarin, was able to restore even a semblance of order. Yet in all the mayhem, Russian administration for the control of Berlin, and control of the German territory they had occupied during their advance, worked with astonishing speed and efficiency.

Even before the fighting ended, a German emigré communist named Walter Ulbricht, together with a group of loyal henchmen, had been flown to the city from Moscow; they now worked flat out to set up the communist machinery in every borough of Berlin, including the sectors that were to be occupied eventually by the western Allies, and — using German labour — stripped the city of everything that was worth dismantling and shipping to the Soviet Union, again paying particular attention to the sectors that were to be turned over to the British and Americans. The French, too, were to have their sector, although this part of the agreement had been reached almost as an afterthought.

It was in February 1945, with German soil yet to be invaded, that the 'Big Three' — Winston Churchill, Josef Stalin and Theodore Roosevelt — had met at Yalta to thrash out an agreement on how the Reich territory was to be occupied once hostilities had ended. This meeting followed one at Quebec in September 1944, when Roosevelt and Churchill had agreed that the British should occupy the north-west of Germany and the Americans the south-west, subject to the Americans having an outlet to the sea at Bremen and Bremerhaven to avoid their lines of communication passing through France.

The machinery of occupation was to be in the hands of a three-power European Advisory Commission, which worked out the fine details of the zoning of Germany and Berlin. The Reich's capital was to be a separate zone, although located in the proposed Soviet Zone, which meant that right of access to it by the Western powers was a primary consideration. The Allied commanders-in-chief were to have supreme authority in their respective zones, and were to exercise joint authority over Germany as a whole, for which purpose they would constitute the Allied Control Council. The administration of Berlin was to be under a joint authority, comprising commandants nominated by the commanders-in-chief.

This plan was broadly approved by the 'Big Three' at Yalta. Stalin had earlier objected to the French participating in the Allied Control Council; he was now persuaded to withdraw his opposition, but only on condition that the French Zone be allocated from the British and American areas of occupation. Surprisingly, there was no specific agreement at Yalta which gave the British and Americans explicit right of access to Berlin from their Zones of Occupation, even though a firm agreement had been reached at Quebec affording the Americans right of passage through the British Zone to the northern German ports.

The debate on whether the Western allies might have reached Berlin before the Russians has been a long and troubled one, and the Supreme Allied Commander in Europe, General Eisenhower, subsequently expressed regrets that he did not change his policy to encompass a powerful thrust towards the German capital. He also made it clear that he would have taken such a decision

Above left *German civilians, their faces masked against the dust and the stench of buried corpses, stand lost and uncertain amid Berlin's ruins. The horrors of the early Soviet occupation are making themselves felt, especially to the women ...*

Above right *A woman pushes her pram through a ruined suburb of Berlin. Note the neatly-stacked pile of bricks. The city's reconstruction has already begun.*

if pressed to do so by the combined Chiefs of Staff. But no such pressure was exerted; the Allies continued to advance on a broad front and halted on the River Elbe, having overrun an area of Germany 400 miles long by 120 miles deep (644 by 193km).

In fact, it would have made no difference to the eventual partition of Germany who reached Berlin first, and Eisenhower's decision probably saved a great many American, British and French lives. There was one other factor: the main reason for the Western Allies' original desire to get to Berlin in a hurry — to take charge of Germany's central administration — no longer existed. The administration of the Reich had long since moved either south to Bavaria or north to Schleswig-Holstein, and the subsequent Anglo-American coup in terms of key personnel rounded up and documents seized was far more spectacular than anything achieved by the Russians.

Nevertheless, the Russians had Berlin, and although it was a hollow, devastated shell of a city it was a prize of supreme importance to them. To most Russians, Germany *was* Berlin, and its capture by Soviet forces, even by default of the Western Allies — which none except the Russian leaders knew about anyway — represented a resounding propaganda success. They showed no desire to share the city with the Western Allies, particularly while they were engaged in stripping it of its remaining booty, and in this attitude they were aided by an unexpected legal obstacle in the path of the planned Allied Control Authority. The Act of Military Surrender, which brought about the capitulation of all German armed forces on 8 May 1945, made no mention of the Allied intention to establish supreme political authority in Germany — in other words, it could possibly be interpreted as not affecting the civil government at all. On 9 May, therefore, the European Advisory Commission had to set to work to devise a legal document giving the Allied powers the civilian authority they required.

While this was going on, the Russians entrenched themselves more deeply in Berlin. Their first priority was to clear away some of the rubble, for it was impossible to administer — and loot — a city whose streets were impassable. Thousands of women, nicknamed *Trümmerfrauen* — women of the rubble — along with children and old men were rounded up and set to work clearing the devastated streets, separating bricks from old mortar and stacking them in piles for future use. If the rebuilding of Berlin — and, for that matter, Germany — was hailed as something of a miracle, then it was achieved in its early stages by

Berlin's Tempelhof Airport pictured in the pre-war heyday of the Third Reich in 1936, soon after it was built.

people such as these, labouring through the months that followed into the bitter winter of 1945-6.

The Russians also paid much attention to repairing airfields in and around Berlin, for use by the 16th Air Army's combat squadrons. It was the 16th Air Army which was to form the Soviet Air Force of Occupation in their zone of Germany, and it maintained a heavy presence. For example, Tempelhof, Berlin's civil airport, was occupied by the Yak-9s of the 515th Fighter Air Regiment and later by other units of the 193rd Fighter Air Division, while the 347th and 518th Fighter Air Regiments moved into Schönefeld and the 265th Fighter Air Division stationed its Lavochkin La-5s at Dalgow.

Typical of the Russian attitude over Berlin, which they had persuaded themselves had been captured as a result of one of the war's decisive battles, was the fact that they insisted on Allied representatives assembling there to accept the German surrender a second time, even though Soviet representatives had been present in Reims when General Eisenhower watched Field-Marshal Jodl put his signature to the Act of Surrender on 7 May. Eisenhower did not attend the signing in Berlin; instead he sent his deputy, Air Chief Marshal Sir Arthur Tedder, at the head of a delegation that included General Carl Spaatz, commander of the US strategic air forces in Europe, and General de Lattre de Tassigny, commander of the French 1st Army. Marshal Georgi K. Zhukov, the Soviet Military Governor of Germany, was to preside over everything.

The Allied delegation flew in from Stendal in three Dakotas, escorted by eighteen Yak- 9s of the 515th Fighter Air Regiment from Tempelhof under the command of Major M.N. Tyulkin. The German delegation also came by air from Flensburg. The American military historian Earl F. Ziemke gives an excellent description of the encounter in his book *Battle for Berlin*, and it is worth repeating here because it gives a good insight into the chaotic conditions that were often to attend meetings with the Soviet authorities in Berlin later, during the crisis of 1948-49.

'The ceremony was scheduled for two o'clock on the afternoon of the 8th. The SHAEF (Supreme Headquarters Allied Expeditionary Force) representative arrived on time, but had to wait several hours for the arrival from Moscow of Zhukov's political advisor, Andrey Y. Vishinsky. By then a second hitch had already developed. The Russians had decorated one wall of the room in which the signing was to take place, a small dining hall in the Karlshorst Military Engineering College in the south-eastern suburbs of Berlin, with the flags of the victors. The flag of France was missing, and de Lattre protested. The Russians, not having a French flag, agreed to make one; but on the first attempt they came up with a Dutch flag.

'After Vishinsky, whom the visitors knew by reputation as the prosecutor at the Soviet purge trials of the 1930s, arrived it appeared for some hours that the signing might not take place at all, at least not in time to have any significance. Zhukov and Tedder had agreed to sign as principals with Spaatz and de Lattre as witnesses, which would have followed a precedent set at Reims where the French Major-General Francois Sevez had signed as a witness. Vishinsky declared that de Lattre might sign to symbolize the revival of France, but that Tedder represented both the British and United States forces and, therefore, Spaatz could not sign. Spaatz insisted on signing if de Lattre did, and the French General declared that he would deserve to be hanged if he returned to France without having put his name on the German capitulation. It was close to seven o'clock at night before the Russians agreed to let both sign — somewhat below the signatures of the principals.

'The ceremony began shortly after eleven and might at times have appeared almost comic had the occasion been a less sombre one. The room was too small to hold comfortably all the officers and newspaper correspondents. Tedder had brought three plane-loads of people with him. Three Soviet generals who arrived late took seats at a small table with three empty chairs — the table reserved for the German delegation — and had to be shooed off. De Lattre impressed the Russians most, mainly because of the cut of his uniform. Spaatz, to them looked irritated and uncomfortable, which he no doubt was.

'After the Soviet and Western representatives were seated, Zhukov gave orders to admit the German delegation, Keitel, Friedeburg, Colonel-General Hans Jürgen Stumpff, representing the Luftwaffe, and a half dozen aides. Keitel wearing a monocle, aroused annoyance with his arrogant demeanour and nonplussed many of those present when he saluted with his Marshal's baton, a gesture which looked as if he were doing an exercise with a dumb- bell. The rest of the Germans were grave, apparently barely able to keep their composure. The signing was completed at about fifteen minutes before midnight. The Germans were the last to sign. After he dismissed the Germans, Zhukov offered souvenir pens to those present in the room, but nobody took any. All of the signatories had used their own pens — except Spaatz and de Lattre who, after arguing long for their right to sign, discovered they had not brought pens ... '

After this somewhat farcical encounter, it was to be two months before the Western Allies once again set foot in Berlin. In the meantime, the first shots were fired in a propaganda war that still goes on today. Soon after the surrender, the Russians began broadcasting from Radio Berlin nineteen hours a day, regaling listeners with programmes of music interspersed with glowing reports on how the Berliners were now attending newly-reopened cinemas and theatres, in between working happily under Soviet direction towards the reconstruction of their city, and other towns and cities in the Soviet-occupied zone. The truth, of course, was rather different, but the Russian approach contrasted sharply with that of the SHAEF-operated Radio Luxembourg, whose output consisted mostly of dull military government announcements and details of Nazi atrocities.

At the end of May, the European Advisory Commission finally produced its reworked document under the heading 'Declaration Regarding the Defeat of Germany and the Assumption of Supreme Authority by the Allied Powers.' It effectively plugged the civil government loophole, but it also contained a number of items that were completely irrelevant, such as ordering all German forces to cease hostilities immediately. 'Probably no nation in history,' says Earl

Above left *The new masters: German civilians raise their hats to a British Occupation Forces officer, who returns their compliment with a salute. The Russians were not so gentlemanly.*

Above right *The rebuilding of Germany: workers manhandle a girder into place during bridge reconstruction, 1946.*

Ziemke with justification, 'has been required to surrender so completely, so abjectly, or so often.'

On 5 June, General Eisenhower, General Bernard Montgomery and General de Lattre went to Berlin to sign the Declaration with their Soviet counterparts. The ceremony took place in the yacht club at Wendenschloss, formerly an exclusive community for top-ranking Nazi officials in the suburbs of Berlin, near a large lakeside villa which had been turned into Marshal Zhukov's residence. The three Western military commanders, under the impression that the signing of the Declaration would mark the official establishment of the Allied Control Council, had brought a large number of staff officers and administrators with them, the intention being that most of these would stay behind and start organizing things.

This illusion, however, was quickly shattered by Zhukov, who refused to allow the Control Council to begin any administrative work until the Allied forces earmarked for the occupation of Germany were in their respective zones. Part of the zone allocated to the Soviet forces, he pointed out, was still occupied by British and American troops. Montgomery informed him that it would take

Above left *One of the biggest problems to beset the governors of the Western Zones was the mass of refugees, fleeing from Soviet-occupied areas in the early weeks after the war.*

Above right *US President Harry S. Truman, whose stance over the Western Allies' rights in Berlin, and against the spread of Communism in Europe, was unwavering.*

three weeks to redeploy them; Zhukov's reaction that this was satisfactory, and would give the commanders time to assemble their Contol Council staffs. The meeting ended with a sumptuous banquet, prepared by the Russians — but they had made no arrangements for the Western representatives to stay in Berlin overnight, and so the transport aircraft flew back to the west before dark.

It was becoming increasingly imperative that the Western Allies establish their foothold in Berlin as quickly as possible, before the Russians began treating the city as their exclusive territory. But there were other problems, not the least of which was that the Russians appeared to be flouting some of the decisions made at Yalta on the occupation of the former Reich territories. For example, without consulting their wartime Allies, they had handed over a large tract of Germany east of the Oder-Neisse Line to Poland, and millions of Germans were driven out. They also set up a provisional government in Austria, which by agreement was to be under four-power control, and made it as difficult as possible for Western missions to enter the country, generally confining them to Vienna.

One man, perhaps, was more aware of impending danger than any other.

Early in June, Winston Churchill wrote to President Truman, who had succeeded Franklin Roosevelt on the latter's death, and suggested that the withdrawal of any forces be postponed until he, Truman and Stalin met at Potsdam in July to reach a firm settlement on a number of questions, particularly the Austrian one. Truman, however, was adamant that the withdrawal of Allied troops from the Soviet Zone must not be used as a bargaining point in relation to other issues; the Allied Control Council could not begin to function until the Americans left the Soviet Zone, and he had been advised that it would harm relations with Russia to postpone action until the Potsdam meeting. Reluctantly, Churchill was obliged to agree.

Both Truman and Churchill wrote to Stalin on 14 and 15 June. Truman proposed that the movement of American troops from the Soviet Zone should begin on the 21st, while Churchill proposed the simultaneous movement of Anglo-American forces into Berlin. Both Western leaders specified that the promotion of free access to Berlin from the British and American Zones by air, rail and road; they also stressed the urgency of settling outstanding problems in Austria. Stalin requested that the date of the Anglo-American move into Berlin be put back until 1 July, as the Russian commanders were to visit Moscow in the meantime and mine clearance operations in the city were not yet completed. Also, he pointed out, the occupation zones of the French forces in both Germany and Austria had yet to be determined. He made no mention of any right of access to Berlin.

Late in June, in response to an American request to carry out a preliminary survey, the Russians agreed to allow passage of a convoy to Berlin. This convoy — designated Preliminary Reconnaissance Party, Berlin — numbered about 100 vehicles and 500 personnel, about half of them belonging to the US military government administration. It was commanded by Colonel Frank L. Howley, head of Military Government Detachment A1A1, as the Berlin detachment was known.

Setting out on 23 June, the convoy ran into problems as soon as it attempted to enter Soviet territory at Dessau, on the Elbe, where it was stopped by the Russians. After several hours of haggling with senior Soviet officers, Howley was finally permitted to cross with fifty vehicles, 37 officers — only four of whom belonged to the military government party — and 175 men. The convoy proceeded under Soviet escort to Babelsberg, where it was placed in a compound under Soviet guard; no-one was allowed to leave, and it eventually returned to the American Zone with its mission unfulfilled. As an indication of things to come, it was hardly encouraging.

On 29 June, Lieutenant-General Lucius Clay, representing General Eisenhower, and Lieutenant-General Sir Ronald Weeks, the British Deputy Military Governor, went to Berlin to discuss the transit arrangement of their respective forces with Marshal Zhukov. Clay later described the meeting:

'We had explained our intent to move into Berlin utilizing three rail lines and two highways and such air space as we needed. Zhukov would not recognize that these routes were essential and pointed out that the demobilization of Soviet forces was taxing existing facilities. I countered that we were not demanding exclusive use of these routes, but merely access over them without restrictions other than the normal traffic control and regulations which the Soviet administration would establish for its own use.

'General Weeks supported my contention strongly. We both knew there was no provision covering access to Berlin in the agreement reached by the European Advisory Commission. We did not wish to accept specific routes which might be interpreted as a denial of our right of access over all routes, but there was a merit to the Soviet contention that existing routes were needed for demobilization purposes. Therefore Weeks and I accepted as a temporary arrangement the allocation of a main highway and rail line and two air corridors, reserving the right to reopen the question in the Allied Control Council. I must admit that we did not then fully realize that the requirement of unanimous consent would enable a Soviet veto in the Allied Control Council to block all of our future efforts.

'While no record was kept at this meeting, I dictated my notes that evening, and they include the following: "It was agreed that all traffic — air, road and rail — would be free from border search or control by customs or military authorities." ... I think now that I was mistaken in not at this time making free access to Berlin a condition to our withdrawal into our occupation zone, but I did not want an agreement in writing which established anything less than the right of unrestricted access.'

Marshal Zhukov had one further point to make. He did not want any kind of formal handover of the Soviet Zone territory about to be evacuated by SHAEF forces. In fact, he requested an interval of two or three miles between the SHAEF rearguard and the Red Army advance guard, just about enough to keep the main forces out of sight of one another. The barriers between East and West were growing stronger.

With this meeting over, Colonel Howley, who had been waiting at Halle with his detachment, now set out for Berlin once more with 85 officers and 136 men. This time, they crossed the Elbe without incident at Dessau, and by nightfall on Sunday 1 July were encamped in the Grünewald, the great expanse of forested parkland on the south-western outskirts of Berlin. Detachment A1A1 was armed and in combat order; Howley was in Berlin and he intended to stay there, come what may.

The Russians were not as co-operative with the British detachment that set out that day to cross the Elbe at Magdeburg en route for Berlin. The British were held up by the Russians, who protested that they had no authority to allow their erstwhile allies through. In any case, they said, all the bridges in Magdeburg were closed for repair. In the end, the British contingent found a bridge the Russians had neglected to guard, and crossed the Elbe over it after a delay of several hours.

The Russians went to considerable lengths to prevent the Americans and British from making a triumphal entry into Berlin with their main occupation forces, scheduled to move on 3 and 4 July. The US 2nd Armored Division, which began its approach march on the 3rd in order to stage an Independence Day parade in Berlin on 4 July, found that the Russians had declared the Elbe bridges at Dessau to be unsafe and had closed the Dessau-Berlin road completely. The division was consequently compelled to make a 65-mile (104 km) detour via Helmstedt.

Meanwhile, the American and British garrison commanders in Berlin, Major-General Floyd L. Parks and Major-General Lewis Lyne, had met with their Russian counterpart Colonel-General Aleksandr V. Gorbatov — who had replaced General Berzarin following the latter's death in a car crash — on 2 July, and had reached agreement that the Western Allies would take over formal control of their sectors at midnight on the 4th. There would be a formal ceremony of occupation; the Russians promised to attend this, and also the parade planned by the Americans.

The parade took place in the afternoon of Independence Day at the Adolf Hitler Barracks. Much of the 2nd Armored Division was still en route, thanks to Soviet intransigence, and the last thing the tired, irritable troops who had reached the city wanted was to take part in a ceremonial function. Food and sleep were much higher on their agenda. To make matters worse, just as the parade was ending General Parks received a message from Zhukov which stated that the western sectors would not be turned over to the Americans and British until the *Kommandatura* (the administrative authority for Berlin, comprising the four commandants) had been properly established.

The British, for their part, had already taken a decision on the matter. Frustrated and annoyed by the delays to which their occupation force had been subjected en route, they had already refused to take over their sector until matters were sorted out. General Parks, however, having failed to make contact with Zhukov, ordered Colonel Howley to deploy his men in the boroughs — Verwaltungsbezirk — of the American sector as planned. When the Russians woke up the next morning, therefore, they found the American flag flying over six boroughs of the American Sector, and it was too late to do anything about it except make protesting noises. Nevertheless, they showed no sign of any willingness to move out and allow the Americans to assume complete control, and to keep the peace the Americans did not insist on such a move for the time being.

The shattered city which the four powers divided between them in July 1945 had a population of about 3,300,000 over 1,000,000 fewer than the pre- war total. It was a city of rubble and splintered fragments of wood where once majestic trees had stood in the parks. It was a city, above all, where no bird sang, a fact that made an indelible impression on the newcomers. That, and the stench of death that drifted from the choked canals and the buried cellars, from the piles of masonry that had once been buildings. The stagnant, scum-covered canals were the breeding places for billions of insects, and the fact that effluent from ruptured sewers had poured into them made the threat of an epidemic very real.

The water mains were broken at 3,000 points; emergency gas and electricity

The two age groups of Berlin — the young and the old, searching for potatoes in a pile of refuse. In 1945, Berlin's population consisted mainly of children and the elderly.

services functioned intermittently; three fire stations out of four had been destroyed. People lived where they could among the ruins under their new overlords, and at this stage the overlords still meant the Russians. Fewer than forty buses, 100 subway cars and a handful of trams drawn by steam engines were the only civilian transport in the city. Berliners were, in theory, allocated a daily food ration amounting to 1,240 calories, but the chaotic distribution system meant that they received only 64 per cent of it. The black market system, already flourishing, took on a new lease of life with the arrival of the Americans, who possessed luxury items unheard of to most Soviet soldiers. Wrist watches, the ultimate in luxury and status to the average Russian, began to exchange hands for as much as $1,000 in Allied Military Marks, the official occupation currency — and the Russians had no shortage of them, for the Western Allies, under pressure, had given the Soviet military administration duplicate plates for printing them. The result was that, while the distribution of marks for the Americans, British and French was strictly controlled, the Russians simply printed as many as they wanted and paid off their troops with them.

The first meeting of the *Kommandatura* — consisting of Generals Gorbatov,

Parks and Lyne, together with their deputies and Brigadier General Jeoffrey de Beauchesne representing France — which had still not been allocated a sector — held its first meeting on 11 July 1945. The main topic of discussion was the provision of food and fuel, which produced an immediate complication; the Russians refused to allow food for the western sectors to be drawn from the Soviet Zone for more than a few days more, and then only on promise of repayment, insisting that there was none to spare and that supplies had to be brought in from western Germany. At the drop of a hat, the British and American commanders now found themselves with close on one and a half million mouths to feed from the scarce resources of the western zones — and the provisions had to be transported over 115 miles (185 km) of Soviet-occupied territory.

At this first meeting of the *Kommandatura*, the Russians insisted that the regulations and procedures they had enforced during their period as sole occupation force in Berlin be retained. The Allies accepted, intending to make changes later after they had had time to make a complete survey of all the conditions prevailing in their sectors. However, as the Russians had the power of veto in the *Kommandatura*, no changes could be made in the pattern of life they had imposed on the city without their consent. As Colonel Howley pointed out later:

'I think it was a good indication of the policy which we were to follow in Berlin for many months, doing almost anything to win over the Russians, allay their suspicions, and convince them we were friends.'

It was a dangerous philosophy to adopt, and one that showed a complete lack of understanding of the Russian mind; for the only attitude the Russian respects at the negotiating table is one of strength. But in the summer of 1945, a strong Allied stance over their rights in Berlin was still three years away.

An old woman collects firewood against the backdrop of ruined Berlin in the spring of 1946.

Chapter Two
Confrontation

To supply the needs of the population of western Berlin, and those of the Allied garrisons — which rose to 20,000 in number during 1946 — the British and Americans were allowed passage for sixteen trains a day, together with road and barge transport. The number of trains allowed to cross the Soviet Zone was later raised to 31. This was sufficient transport to provision the western sectors of the city.

The initial problem, however, lay in the fact that the necessary supplies were simply not available in the western zones. Western Germany had always been the heartland of the nation's industry in modern times; it was the eastern part of the country, now under Soviet domination, that had traditionally been Germany's granary. This geographical division caused major problems when it came to reparations; at Potsdam, the agreement had been that reparations payments were to leave the German people with enough resources to exist without external assistance, but since the Soviet Zone was mainly agricultural and the Russians needed machinery and plant, the agreement permitted the Soviet Union to receive an additional fifteen per cent of the surplus capital equipment from the western zones in exchange for food and other commodities, plus an extra ten per cent without any payment or exchange.

The Potsdam Agreement had made provision for Germany to be treated as a single economic unit, with an equal distribution of essential goods between the various zones. Sufficient plant was to be maintained to keep the economy going; Germany was to be made to pay for the Second World War, but not at the cost of a starving population.

That was the principle. In practice, nothing worked. First of all, the French — who were not invited to be present at Potsdam, an omission they regarded as insulting — did everything in their power to block the creation of an administrative system controlled by Germans. They did this from a position of some strength, because their zone was able to support itself economically. Secondly, the Russians showed an early determination to bleed Germany white, regardless of what had been agreed at Potsdam. They steadfastly refused to pool their zonal surplus, and continued to draw reparations from production. It was an extremely unfair situation; while the Russian Zone, like that of the French, was self-supporting, the British and American Zones were not. Their essential supplies had to be imported, mainly from the United States, and paid for; this added to Britain's own severe post-war economic problems, starved as she was of currency, and to make matters worse her zone, which encompassed the Ruhr, was the most densely populated of all.

For the German people in the west, the time that would go down in history as 'Der Grosse Hunger' — the Great Famine — was beginning. The minimum daily calorie intake to ensure survival and enough energy for work is 2,300. On paper, the Allied military administration in Germany reduced this to a bare minimum of 1,500. But in 1946 the German people were not even getting this. In the British Zone the daily ration allocation produced an intake of 1,040 calories, in the American Zone 1,275. And in the vengeful French Zone, light workers received 927 and heavy workers 1,144. These figures were also reflected in the western sectors of Berlin.

The outcome was inevitable. In the three western zones, and in western Berlin, manual workers were using their reserves of fat and there was no intake to replace them, with the result that muscles began to deteriorate. The consequence of this chronic undernourishment was that on average, production dropped by twenty per cent in Germany's industrial cities. Doctors reported a frightening increase in tuberculosis and other illnesses, and a rise in sickness affecting the central nervous system.

Self-sufficiency in the western zones was a myth. In the British Zone alone, 28,000 farms had been destroyed in the closing weeks of the war. Only the co-operation of the Soviet Union could have alleviated the situation, and such co-operation was not forthcoming. The figures speak for themselves. Before the occupation, the territories now under Soviet domination had provided the German population with one-third of the nation's farm produce. In 1939, in the areas of western Germany now controlled by the Americans, British and French, 272 people had been able to survive on the produce of 247 acres (100 hectares) of land; in 1946, the same area had to produce food for 318 people. Also whereas the western areas had provided accommodation for 58 per cent of the total German population in 1939, that figure had now risen to seventy per cent in 1946 — a result of the headlong flight from the east ahead of the advancing Russian armies.

It was a recipe for disaster; a vicious circle in which the Germans starved because they could not produce enough, and could not produce enough because they were starving. Between 1 January 1946 and 20 June 1948, 143,000 people — one-third of all deaths registered — died from exhaustion and malnutrition in the cities of western Germany. In Hamburg, between 1 July and 19 October 1946, for every person hospitalized with hunger-related illnesses there were 48 known cases who were not admitted to hospital. In September of that year, 13,000 people became hospital patients in the

Opposite *When the Allies entered Germany they found devastation everywhere in the Reich's industrial heartland. Yet in the months after the war, the burden of reparations — one of the early causes of the rift between East and West — gave the Germans little chance to rebuild their wrecked industry and produce in order to survive.*

Düsseldorf area suffering from malnutrition; but 25,000 more were not admitted because there were no beds.

In the latter half of 1946, the British and Americans proposed a possible solution. Britain's Foreign Minister, Ernest Bevin — a key figure in Clement Attlee's recently-elected Labour Government — agreed with James F. Byrnes, the US Director of War Mobilization and Reconversion, General Clay and the American political advisor in Germany, Robert Murphy, that an economic merger of the American and British Zones would be advantageous. While the two zones were separately controlled, bureaucracy made it hard, if not impossible, for the heavy industries of the British Zone to provide the raw materials needed by the manufacturing industries in the American Zone. The French, predictably, refused to have anything to do with the idea, while the Russians were highly critical of it.

Byrnes and Bevin decided that they were going to proceed, with or without the co-operation of the Russians. Nevertheless, a formal offer was made to them by the Control Council, with General Clay as the spokesman, on 18 July 1946:

'Since the zones of Germany are not self-supporting of themselves and since treating two zones or more as an economic unit would better this situation in the zones concerned, the United States representatives in Germany will join with the representatives of any other occupying power or powers in measures to treat their respective zones as an economic unit, pending four-power agreement to carry out the Potsdam provision regarding the treatment of all Germany as an economic unit and the reaching of a balanced economy throughout Germany.'

The American standpoint on the matter had been summed up a week earlier by General George C. Marshall, the US Secretary of State:

'The United States Government does not want a piece of vengeance and it is convinced that the economic recovery of Germany along peaceful lines is necessary to the economic revival of Europe. It desires the denazificaton of Germany which will encourage democratic forces who otherwise may feel they cannot exert themselves with a fair chance. The sure way to encourage the growth of democratic forces in Germany is to state in definite terms the conditions of settlement, to fix German disarmament measures and the reparations which it must pay. The German people will then realize that the harder they work the sooner they will be allowed to share in the benefits of European recovery. Germany's future boundaries should likewise be defined so that the German people may know that, as long as they adhere to the settlement, no interference will be given to their reconstruction efforts, which will help both themselves and all of Europe.

'While controls and security forces must remain for a long time in Germany, mass occupation and military government continued over a long period could defeat our own purposes. The German people must have the opportunity to minimize the certain difficulties and hardships of their situation by their own efforts so that they will learn not to blame their trials on Allied occupation but rather, and properly, on the devastating war of aggression which their leaders let loose.'

The planned Anglo-American 'Bizone' came into existence on 1 January 1947. Before that, in the autumn of 1946, General Clay and the British Military Governor, Sir Brian Robertson, had set up German committees to be responsible for economics, food and agriculture, transport, communications, the civil service and finance — all, of course, subject to the overall supervision of the military authorities. At a later date, a German Economic Council was brought into being at Frankfurt; it consisted of 52 members, elected by the existing *Landtage* or State legislatures, and it was the first time that Germany had witnessed a democratically elected governing body since the days of the Weimar Republic. For the time being, its function was to advise; the Control Council remained the overriding authority. But it was an essential first step towards the eventual formation of an autonomous Federal German Government.

As early as January 1947, Clay and Robertson were anticipating the eventual breakup of the Allied Control Council, although they reaffirmed the intention of the United States and Britain to participate in it. At the same time, anticipating problems that might arise in the four-power control of Berlin, they indicated that the Western Allies would remain in the city 'regardless of any Soviet pressures'. The question of currency reform was also raised by General Clay, who strongly advocated the issue of a new and separate currency for the British and American Zones.

The currency question was raised by the Foreign Ministers of the occupying powers at a meeting held in Moscow in March 1947. It produced a sharp reaction from the Russians, whose opinion, voiced in the pages of *Izvestia*, was that 'The new monetary unit is to fulfil the function of a golden chain forcibly linking Germany with the notorious Western bloc'. Yet something clearly had to be done, for the continued circulation of Hitler's Reichsmark, with its wayward and unco-ordinated exchange rates, was having a chaotic effect on German exports; even the Russians agreed with that, and for the time being went along with an Anglo-American plan for the conversion of Reichsmarks into the new currency — Deutschemarks — over a period of a year or so.

Oddly enough, the main bone of contention in 1947 centred not on the structure of the new currency, but on where it was to be printed. The Russians wanted to print it in Leipzig, but the Americans — mindful that the Leipzig printing works had produced millions of near-perfect counterfeit £5 notes during the war, and of the Russians' wholesale printing of occupation currency, wanted the printing to be done simultaneously in Berlin and Leipzig, under strict control. The argument continued throughout the year, and in the meantime inflation ran riot.

Meanwhile, events in Germany were becoming incidental to what was happening elsewhere in Europe in the light of Soviet expansion. First of all, the Russians had annexed the Baltic States, along with parts of Finland, Poland, Czechoslovakia, Romania — and, of course, Germany. In 1945 they had begun to involve themselves in the civil war in Greece. Wherever the presence of their armed forces enabled them to apply direct pressure, they insisted upon

Communist agents participating in the government — a policy that was apparent in the Soviet Zone of Germany — even though the first post-war election had everywhere shown that the Communists represented only a minority.

In 1947, the movement gathered speed. The Communist Party seized power in Hungary, after forcing the resignation of the Nagy Government; in Bulgaria, where the leader of the opposition, Petkov, was hanged; in Romania, where Maniu, leader of the peasant party, was condemned to life imprisonment; and finally in Poland, where Mikolajczyk, also the leader of the peasant opposition, had to flee to the West. There remained Czechoslavakia, where the regime, though still democratic, maintained the most friendly relations with the USSR. In February 1948, however, a Soviet plot brought about the capitulation of President Benes, who handed over power to the Communists.

Within this framework of expansion, Soviet intentions in Germany became increasingly clear. The Soviet Union desired nothing less than a new centralized German government — but one within the framework of the growing Communist satellite system. Only then could the Russians begin to feel secure in the face of German resurgence, and against a backdrop of twenty million of their people slaughtered between 1941 and 1945, it is not difficult to appreciate their point of view.

In 1947, both the Russians and the Western Allies still regarded Berlin as the nerve-centre of a centralized Germany. To the Russians, control of the city somehow symbolized control of the German will; to the Western Allies, control of the city, or at least part of it, became increasingly important as part of the overall plan to establish a new and democratic freedom in the areas under their authority.

As far as controlling the German will was concerned, the Russians had begun to run into trouble when they tried to bring about a merger between their protégé Communist Party in Berlin and the Social Democratic Party, one of the four embryo political parties which the Russians had allowed to come into being in Berlin in June 1945. (Apart from the Communists, the other parties were the Christian Democrats and Liberal Democrats). In May 1946, 25,000 Berliners belonging to the SDP turned out to vote in a referendum; it was held only in the western sectors of the city, because the Russians closed down the polling booths in their own sector at the last minute, but the result was an overwhelming rejection of their aims; 82 per cent of the voters wanted nothing to do with the Communists. In the Eastern Sector, where SDP members had been subjected to a great deal of intimidation, Walther Ulbricht's Communists proceeded to ignore the outcome of the referendum and merged with those Social Democrats under Russian control to form a new party, the Amalgamated Workers' Party (SED).

Despite this clear warning, the Russians agreed, together with the other three powers, to allow full elections to take place in the autumn of 1946 to choose a municipal parliament, which was to have 130 members. Electioneering was blatant in the extreme, inducements in the form of cigarettes, liquor and clothing being distributed by all the occupying powers. Election literature was unsubtle, too. One particularly effective poster read: 'Were you raped by a Russian? Vote for the SED.' The poster was issued by the Christian Democrats.

The Social Democrats won 47 per cent of the vote, the CDU 21 per cent, the Liberal Democrats nine per cent and the Communist SED 19 per cent. However, the jubilation at the Russians' discomfiture quickly turned sour, for it was the Russians who had the last word.

Shortly after they occupied Berlin, and before the Western Allies arrived, the Russians had compelled thousands of skilled workers to sign a declaration to the effect that they would, under certain conditions, agree to work in the Soviet Union. Within 48 hours of the elections, the deportations started. During the days that followed, 25,000 skilled workers and their families were forcibly removed to other locations in the Soviet Zone and farther afield. Protests by the Western Allies were to no avail; the Russians simply vetoed everything. Probably for the first time, the citizens of west Berlin, who had been so glad to see the arrival of the Americans and British, realized fully how slender and insecure their 100-odd-mile (160 km) lifeline with the Western Zones really was. In Berlin, the bitter winter of 1946-7 was a despondent one, a microcosm of 'Der Grosse Hunger' compounded by conditions in which thousands of people ran a real danger of freezing to death, and where ten per cent of all hospital beds were occupied by pneumonia cases.

In March 1947, the United States at last took the first step to halt the spread of Communism in Europe. The main areas of concern were Greece and Turkey, both of which were threatened by political and economic collapse. Under the terms of what was called the Truman Doctrine, the USA extended military and economic aid to both these countries. In effect, President Truman, with the support of Congress, was affirming a United States policy of supporting free peoples who were resisting attempted subjugation by armed minorities or by outside pressures; a balance of power was being created with the aim of containing Communism, and its immediate effect was to be most clearly seen in divided Berlin.

The second key point of the Truman Doctrine was a firm promise of material aid to ailing Europe under the terms of the Marshall Plan, named after General Marshall, the US Secretary of State. Marshall, speaking at Harvard on 5 June 1947, made it clear that American policy was directed not against any country or doctrine, but against hunger, poverty, desperation and chaos. It provided, in effect, a much softer and more reconciliatory follow-up to the first part of the Truman Doctrine, and invited the co-operation of the Soviet Union.

On 26 June, the British and French Foreign Ministers called a meeting in Paris to discuss the Marshall Plan and make arrangements for the formal inauguration of the Organization for European Economic Co-operation (OEEC). The Soviet Foreign Minister, Vyacheslav Molotov, also attended, but it was a matter of pure diplomacy that he did so; ten days earlier, the Communist Party newspaper *Pravda* had already denounced the Marshall Plan as an American bid to exert political pressure in the affairs of other countries, backed up by dollars.

On 2 July, after a good deal of manoeuvring, the Russian delegation withdrew from the Paris talks, having done its best to disrupt them, and the Soviet Government forbade all East European countries within its sphere of influence to accept aid under the Marshall Plan. It was a very shrewd and calculated political decision, and its implications were quite clear. If the United States now went ahead and offered aid to Western Europe, and the Europeans accepted, the result would be a complete political, economic and military division of the continent from northern Norway to the Black Sea. The division — Winston Churchill's oft-quoted 'Iron Curtain' — would effectively create two separate nations in Germany, with the Russians in full and unchallenged control of the eastern part. It was precisely what the Russians wanted. If they could not exercise domination over the whole of Germany, nor prevent the foundation of a democratic German State under the supervision of the Western Allies, they could at least hold the Eastern Zone firmly behind the barrier they had created along the Elbe.

Yet, in the summer of 1947, the thinking of the Soviet Government was that perhaps the Western Allies might be compelled to abandon their plans for the Western Zones of Germany after all. It was a matter of exerting maximum pressure on a point where the Allies were at their most isolated and vulnerable: Berlin. If the Western powers could be compelled to evacuate Berlin, their prestige in Germany — and throughout the world — would suffer a terrible blow. The question uppermost in the Russian mind was, what price were the Western powers prepared to pay in order to retain their sectors unmolested? Would they, for example, be prepared to abandon their scheme for the revival of Western Germany as a nation in its own right? Either way, the Russians would have won a bloodless victory of great magnitude.

The preliminary skirmishes began in 1947, when the Russians tried to discredit the City Assembly by refusing to countenance the newly-elected Chief Bürgmeister, Ernst Reuter, who had been chosen by the Social Democrats. Correspondence addressed to him at the City Hall, which was in the Soviet Zone, was returned with the comment that there was no such person. The principal problem with Reuter, in the eyes of the Russians, was that he had once been a Communist but that he had since renounced Communism, having become thoroughly disillusioned with the demands of Moscow, and become a Socialist. The Russian objection to Reuter was overcome, for the time being, by Reuter himself, who stepped down and allowed a woman, Frau Louise Schroeder, to act as his representative.

Born in Altona, Hamburg, in 1887, Louise Schroeder was the tenth child of a builder's labourer and grew up in conditions of appalling poverty. Somehow she fought her way out of her environment and became a top-grade secretary. After the First World War she was one the the 37 women delegates to the Social Democratic Party's first congress, and was later elected to the Reichstag. A formidable character, she was recognized as a possible source of danger to the Nazi regime, and compelled to report twice daily to the police. With Berlin under Soviet domination she resisted all blandishments to join the Communist

Key figures in the civil administration of Berlin during the Airlift: Louise Schroeder and Ernst Reuter.

SED. She was elected to the post of acting Mayor in May 1947, and in the eighteen months she was to hold that position this small, bespectacled and very tough woman was to prove herself a godsend to the Berliners time after time.

The Russians' tactics in Berlin during 1947 were designed primarily to create as much tension as possible. They deliberately spread rumours that the Western Allies were about to pull out; they kidnapped active anti-Communists from the western sectors; they allowed armed Russian soldiers to run riot, and some of them were shot by American MPs who had been alerted by the virtually powerless civilian police. The British MPs used somewhat different tactics, preferring to disarm any wayward Russians, beat them senseless and throw them back into their own sector. Other harassments involved the arrest, in the Soviet sector, of Berliners carrying western sector newspapers; normal railway passenger services entering Berlin were subjected to increasingly interminable delays, and cars from the west were forbidden to enter the Soviet Zone unless the drivers carried special permits, which needless to say were extremely difficult to obtain.

In May 1947 a new British Commandant arrived in Berlin. He was Major-General E.O. Herbert, and he was far from prepared for what he encountered when he got there. He had, of course, received all the proper briefings on denazification and the rest, of the need to exercise complete authority over the vanquished Germans, and he was quite confident that he would be able to work well with the Russians, who after all were soldiers like himself. It did not take long for him to alter his opinion.

He found that in two years of joint occupation, the Russians had agreed to virtually nothing worthwhile concerning the city's administration. There was, however, one exception. Relaxing their earlier stand, the Russians had agreed to Berlin being served by three air corridors, subject to the restrictions of passage over the Soviet Zone imposed by the Quadripartite Agreement of November 1945. Each corridor was twenty statute miles wide (32 km), extending vertically from ground level to 10,000 ft (3,048 m). Two terminated in the British Zone, leading to Hamburg and Hannover, and one in the American Zone, leading to Frankfurt. The two terminating in the British Zone passed over comparatively flat country, the highest point of which was some 400 ft (122 m) above ground level, whereas the Frankfurt corridor crossed high ground — rising to 3,000 ft (914 m) close to the corridor's boundaries — over much of its length. The Hamburg corridor crossed 95 miles (153 km) of the Soviet Zone from Berlin to the nearest point of the British Zone; the Hannover corridor was 117 miles (188 km) long and the Frankfurt corridor 216 (347 km). No radio or radar navigation aids were available in Soviet-occupied territory.

All three corridors terminated in the Berlin Control Zone, a circular area of twenty statute miles (32 km) radius from 52°30'N, 13°22'E — centred on the Allied Control Council's building — about half of it over the Soviet Sector of Berlin. All British, American and French aircraft had freedom of passage within this Zone, except in the restricted areas surrounding the Soviet military airfields at Staaken, Schönewalde and Johannisthal.

The terminus for British aircraft flying into Berlin was Gatow, which was originally developed by the Luftwaffe as a training centre and was considered roughly to be the equivalent of the Royal Air Force College, Cranwell. During the war it was used as a fighter base. It had no runways, and one of the first tasks after the RAF took it over in 1945 was to lay a 4,500 ft (1,370m) pierced steel planking (PSP) runway to handle the limited number of Avro Anson and Douglas Dakota traffic and the operation of eight Tempest Mk V fighter-bombers of No 3 Squadron, which left for Dedelstorf in May 1946. The PSP runway proved inadequate on the sandy soil, and a concrete runway designed for medium-sized aircraft was started in 1947.

In fact, the renewal of the runway at Gatow was part of a plan, drawn up by the Director of Air Support and Transport Operations — Air Commodore David Atcherley — at the Air Ministry and HQ RAF Transport Command at Bushey Park for the emergency supply of the British garrison in Berlin in the event of a major crisis developing. At that time, however, there was no thought at all of feeding or supplying the German citizens of Berlin itself.

The American air terminus in Berlin, Templehof, had been designed before the war as Berlin's principal civil airport and had some magnificent buildings, including a massive operations and administration block with seven storeys underground. During the war years, this remarkable structure housed, among other things, a Messerschmitt factory and a well-equipped hospital. When the

USAF took the site over following a brief Soviet occupation, they laid a 4,987 by 120-ft (1,520 by 36 m) PSP runway, together with an apron and connecting taxiway built of concrete block.

As 1947 moved towards winter, conditions in Berlin had improved a little, but not much. Food was still desperately short, and a 'luxury' dinner during those months might consist of a plate of thin vegetable soup, two small potatoes, forty grammes of meat, one slice of black bread, and five grammes of margarine, the whole totalling 700 calories and washed down with a cup of ersatz coffee. It was small wonder that the barter system and the black market functioned almost unchecked, despite Louise Schroeder's strenuous efforts to stamp out this kind of illegal trading; the Germans wanted the luxuries that could be provided by the Allies, and they were prepared to pay for them with whatever they had. Many British and American servicemen grew wealthy during their tour in Berlin, and for that matter anywhere else in Germany, and in the Russian Sector rape was no longer necessary in an environment where a woman would sell herself for a bar of chocolate. In the winter of 1947-48, the daily ration for civilians in the western sectors of Berlin amounted to one pint of skimmed milk, one pound of potatoes, 35 grammes of vegetables, three slices of bread, 20 grammes of fat, 30 grammes of meat, 4.5 grammes of cheese, a piece of lump sugar, 20 grammes of other essential items such as salt — and on special occasions an egg. This 1,000-calorie package was still the daily ration six months later. A pound of butter was a luxury costing 250 Marks (NB, 1lb = 0.4536 Kg; 1 gramme = 0.0022 lb.)

German women returning to their Berlin homes after a successful foraging expedition.

At the beginning of 1948, it was becoming increasingly apparent that the Russians were going to step up their pressure on the Allied foothold in Berlin. Incidents in the city multiplied, and on 24 January Russian security guards stopped a British military train at the border and detached two coaches containing German passengers. A fortnight later, having ignored British protests about this incident, an American military train was stopped in similar manner and German civilian passengers were forced to submit to a humiliating search. The Russians were now insisting on the right to board all trains entering the Soviet Zone in order to check the identity of individual passengers; if they met with opposition, the trains were simply shunted into sidings and held there for hours. Freight trains were stopped on the pretext that their cargoes had to be examined, piece by piece, for contraband. On one occasion the Americans sent out a train with armed guards to see if the Russians would attempt to use force to stop it, but the Russians were much more subtle than that; they just switched it electrically into a siding and left it there for several hours until it went back the way it had come. Road traffic was also halted on the Berlin autobahn, usually on the pretext that the road needed repairing, and forced either to turn back or make unnecessary detours. Other vehicles were turned back because their drivers were alleged to have irregular passes, yet they would be allowed through the Helmstedt checkpoint with no trouble the next day, with exactly the same documents. More often than not, this harassment was directed at vehicles heading from Berlin to the Western Zones, and the crude Russian psychological message was clear. Not only can we prevent you from reaching Berlin, they were saying; we can also prevent you from leaving it.

The harassment and the resulting tension continued throughout the early weeks of 1948. Then, in March, the Russians left the Western powers in no doubt about their intention to isolate Berlin. Their move came in the wake of a conference of West European Foreign Ministers which was held in London on 6 March to discuss, among other topics, the possibility of forming a separate government for Western Germany — a prospect which the Russians viewed with alarm, for a German State outside Soviet control had no place in their long-term plans for Europe.

On 20 March, a meeting of the Allied Control Council was held in Berlin, and Marshal Vassily Sokolovsky, the Soviet Military Governor, launched into the attack straight away, protesting that the London conference, although it had discussed important matters affecting the future of Germany, had been called without the knowledge of the Control Council and that the Russians had not been informed of any consequent directive issued to the Western military governors. General Clay and General Sir Brian Robertson replied that they had received no directive, as the London conference had no power to issue one, and reminded Sokolovsky that the Russians were keeping the Control Council in the dark about events in the Soviet Zone.

The Soviet intention to provoke a confrontation in the Control Council became clear when Sokolovsky produced a prepared statement in which he stated that the British and American delegations were wrecking the control

Left to right: the British, French and US Military Governors in Germany, General Sir Brian Robertson, General Pierre Koenig and General Lucius D. Clay, in conversation during the ceremony in Frankfurt to mark the creation of a West German State, 1 July 1948.

administration in Germany and must bear the responsibility for it. 'By their actions,' he went on, 'these delegations once again confirm that the Control Council virtually exists no longer as the supreme authority in Germany. This constitutes one of the most serious violations of the obligations devolving on the British, American and French authorities in Germany by virtue of the four-power agreements on the administration of Germany during the occupation period. It is therefore clear that the actions which are being taken now, or will be taken in the future, following the unilateral decision of the London conference, cannot be recognized as lawful.'

Clay and Robertson were given no opportunity to reply to this statement. As soon as he had finished, Sokolovsky swept his papers together and walked out, followed by his entourage, without setting a date for the next meeting.

The Russians followed up this move by postponing other administrative meetings which were due to be held at a lower level, although they did attend a regular meeting of the *Kommandatura* on 24 March. As usual, nothing of importance was discussed. Meanwhile, the Russians made strenuous attempts to interfere with the proceedings of the City Assembly and stepped up their propaganda war against the Western zones. On 26 March, Lieutenant-General G. Lukyanchenko, the Soviet Chief of Staff, accused the Western powers of aiding and abetting illegal traffic into Berlin, and four days later he stated that steps would have to be taken to protect the inhabitants of the city against 'subversive and terrorist elements'.

Things were beginning to escalate rapidly now. On 31 March, Lieutenant-General Mikhail Dratvin, the Soviet Deputy Military Governor in Berlin, informed his Western colleagues that from 1 April all Western nationals travelling to the city via the autobahn and railway would be required to show their identity documents at Soviet control points, and submit to a luggage inspection. Furthermore, Soviet permits would be required for all military freight leaving and entering the city. The British and Americans, realizing that the Russians were not bluffing, suspended all military passenger trains, replacing them with bus and air transport. The French followed suit a day later after the Russians removed more than sixty German passengers from one of their Berlin-bound trains.

The Russians also extended their restrictions to parcel mail leaving Berlin and to waterway traffic. Barge captains were told that they needed new papers to enter the Soviet Zone, but they were not told what sort of papers were required or where to apply for them. In this respect the Russians outfoxed themselves, because much of the cargo that was subjected to lengthy delay was destined for Russia, the Soviet Zone and Czechoslovakia.

On 3 April the Russians closed secondary rail routes from Hamburg and Frankfurt and demanded that all rail traffic be funnelled through Helmstedt. As the Allies had already suspended the loading of military freight in Berlin, this meant that all military rail traffic between the city and the Western Zones was now at a virtual standstill. All this produced a flurry of correspondence between the Western Allies and the Soviet authorities, the main gist of which was that the Russians were illegally denying the British, Americans and French their right of unrestricted access to Berlin. The Russians argued that no such agreement concerning the right of unrestricted access was in existence.

They were right, in the sense that there was no written agreement. All that existed was the verbal agreement reached three years earlier with Marshal Zhukov. Brigadier-General C.K. Gailey, acting for the US authorities, tried to set matters on a firmer footing in a letter to General Dratvin:

'The agreement under which we entered Berlin clearly provided for our free and unrestricted utilization of the established corridors. This right was a condition precedent to our entry into Berlin and our final evacuation of Saxony and Thuringia. I do not consider that the provisions you now propose are consistent with this agreement. I must also advise you that we do not propose to accept changes in this agreement.'

Gailey did offer some concessions, offering to allow Soviet officials to check passenger and freight manifests on condition that they did not actually board any train. He was also prepared to enter into further discussions, provided that these were not called at short notice. Dratvin, however, remained adamant.

'There was not, nor can there be, any agreement concerning disorderly and uncontrolled traffic of freight and personnel through the territory of the Soviet Zone. It is obvious that such disorderly and uncontrolled traffic could only lead to confusion, and would contribute to provoking unrest in the Soviet Zone through which traffic between Berlin and the Western Zones is passing. You are without doubt aware of the many facts which show that the lack of control has been used by shady individuals for all kinds of illegal operations, as well as by criminal and other restless elements, causing lawlessness and a condition of crime on the territory of the Soviet Zone of Occupation. This constitutes a threat to the general peace.'

On 6 April Ernest Bevin, the British Foreign Secretary, summed up the prevailing situation in a statement to Parliament. 'It should be explained,' he said, 'that the regulations for travel to and from Berlin are not so clearly specified [as the terms of the four-power agreement for the occupation of the city]. When the arrangements were made a good deal was taken on trust between the Allies, and until this event travel has been reasonably satisfactory. On the roads British travellers have shown their documents. On military trains this has not been required, since the trains were supplied by, and were under the exclusive control of the British military authorities. The new difficulty results from the Soviet demand that Soviet military personnel should board the trains and examine passengers' documents.'

Bevin stated that the British Government would welcome further discussions leading to an agreement. However, Britain would not yield her right to free access to her sectors in the divided city.

Uppermost in the minds of the Western leaders, both civil and military, was what would happen if the Russians used military force to back their demands. One thing was clear from the outset. Berlin could not be defended. General Lucius Clay, the Military Governor in Germany and commander of the US forces in Europe, had only 6,500 troops in the Berlin area, and they were outnumbered three to one by the Russians. Instructed by the US Joint Chiefs of Staff to avoid the use of force at all costs, Clay's immediate preoccupation lay in finding an immediate means of supplying the garrison and the civilian population of the western sectors of Berlin should the road and rail links be severed completely.

To test the feasibility of forging an air supply link with Berlin, Clay ordered the 61st Troop Carrier Group at Rhein-Main Air Base, near Frankfurt, to begin flying in supplies with effect from 2 April aboard its 25 Douglas C-47 transport aircraft, each of which could carry up to three tons of cargo. This operation encountered no opposition from the Russians, but on 5 April there was an indication of what might happen in the future when a Vickers Viking airliner of British European Airways, on a scheduled flight to Berlin, was buzzed by a Soviet Yak-3 fighter as it approached the capital in one of the recognized air corridors. The Russian fighter made one pass, turned to make another, and collided head-on with the airliner. Both aircraft crashed, the Russian being killed along with ten passengers and crew in the Viking.

In the air, too, the Soviet forces of occupation had overwhelming numerical air superiority. The commander of the United States Air Forces in Europe, General Curtis LeMay — who had taken over from the USAF's first commander, Brigadier General John McBain, in October 1947 — had only eleven operationally effective combat groups with some 275 aircraft, mostly A-

The most common fighter type encountered by Airlift crews was the Yakovlev Yak-3. During the Airlift, the Russians moved additional squadrons into Eastern Zone airfields.

The most potent RAF fighter serving with the British Air Forces of Occupation in the early days of the airlift was the Hawker Tempest F Mk 2, which equipped Nos 16, 26 and 33 Squadrons (No 135 Wing) at Gutersloh.

26 light bombers and F-47 Thunderbolts and F-51 Mustang fighters. In the British Zone, the RAF had a few squadrons of Mosquitos, Spitfires and Tempests; the latter were the most potent piston-engined fighters in service anywhere in the world, but there were only three squadrons of them in the British Air Forces of Occupation.

Against this, the Soviet Air Force had a tactical air force of some 4,000 aircraft in eastern Europe, about two-thirds of it with the 16th Air Army in Germany. The equipment comprised piston-engined types such as the Il-10 Shturmovik, the Yak-3 and La-9 fighters, and Pe-2 and Tu-2 light bombers. The Soviet Air Force also had an embryo strategic bombing capability in a small but growing force of Tupolev Tu-4 bombers, copies of the Boeing B-29 Superfortress, several examples of which had been forced down in Russia after bombing raids against the Japanese during World War 2. In addition, the Russians were known to be introducing a swept-wing jet interceptor, the MiG-15, to their first-line fighter units early in 1948 — and the Western Allies in Europe had nothing to compare with that. Its American equivalent, the F-86A Sabrejet, had yet to enter squadron service in the USA.

LeMay determined that if war did result from a struggle for possession of

Above *Shturmoviks were also encountered frequently, carrying out air-to-ground firing exercises on ranges below the air corridors.*

Below *Together with the Tupolev Tu-2, the Petlyakov Pe-2 was the principal Soviet light bomber in service with the 16th Air Army in the Eastern Zone.*

Berlin, he would do his best to meet it with the scant resources available. His first concern was to protect the vital supply line between the American Zone and Bremerhaven, which was prone to a sudden Russian armoured thrust, and so as an initial step he created a defence in depth by organizing a series of air bases well to the west of the Rhine in France and Belgium. The Chiefs of Staff of the French and Belgian Air Forces, Generals Charles Lecheres and Lucien Leboutte, readily agreed to this plan and made several of their airfields available for American air reinforcement.

Quietly and by devious methods, the bases were stockpiled with bombs, fuel and spare parts, and 200 USAF ground crew in civilian clothing were assigned to each base. Consequently, by the end of April 1948 LeMay had a string of operational airfields at his disposal, ready to receive combat aircraft reinforcements if the Russians made a hostile move.

April and May passed relatively quietly in Berlin, apart from the continued Soviet propaganda barrage and further traffic restrictions. Discussions on the formation of a West German Government continued in London, and on 7 June it was announced that this would be created within a year, with a federal constitution being drafted in September. The announcement was, to all intents and purposes, a slap in the face for the Russians, and they were swift in their reaction. On 15 June, they closed the autobahn bridge over the Elbe at Magdeburg for repairs, forcing all traffic to go via the ferry and adding an hour and a half to the road journey.

The next day, after thirteen long hours of fruitless discussion in the *Kommandatura*, Colonel Frank Howley, the American Commandant, suddenly announced that he was tired and that he was going home to bed. As he rose, an advisor whispered something in the ear of General Kotikov, the Soviet Commandant. Kotikov stood up and announced that the Americans had broken up the *Kommandatura*, and that the Russians were leaving. General Ganeval, the French Commandant, who had been presiding, objected that the date of the next meeting had not been settled.

'As far as I am concerned,' retorted Kotikov as he stalked out, 'there will be no next meeting.'

Only one thing remained common to the four zones of occupation; the continued circulation of the outdated Reichsmark, and the hyper-inflation that went along with it. Then, on Friday 18 June 1948, the Western Allies, who had been making their preparations in great secrecy, dropped their bombshell. At a major press conference in Frankfurt, the British and Americans announced that a new currency, the Deutschemark, would replace the Reichsmark in the Western Zones from Sunday, 20 June. The currency, said the Allies, would be backed not by gold but by 'the German people's industry, their tradition of hard work, and the promise of Marshal Aid'.

On that same Friday, General Robertson wrote to Marshal Sokolovsky: 'I recognize the special circumstances of quadripartite government in Berlin and have no wish to disturb it unless this becomes unavoidable. As you know, we have striven for many months to reach a quadripartite agreement on a currency and financial reform which would apply to the whole of Germany. I am still firmly convinced that the only satisfactory course is to have financial reform on an all-German basis. Meanwhile, the economy of the British Zone is suffering acutely from the evils of inflation and economic stagnation, which our quadripartite proposals for financial reform were designed long ago to eradicate. I feel that I am not justified in waiting any longer before taking remedial measures. I have therefore decided to include the British Zone in a scheme of currency reform to be introduced into the Western Zones on Sunday, 20 June. Advance copies of the relevant laws will be sent to you.'

The issue of the Deutschemark amounted to an admission by the Allies that the division of Germany was complete, and it was the final nail in the coffin of four-power government. That evening, the Russians stopped all passenger traffic from West Germany by both road and rail and forbade all pedestrians, motorists and rail passengers to cross into the Soviet Zone from midnight. Then, on 20 June, they stopped an American military train at Marienborn and pulled up some of the track ahead of it.

At midnight on 23 June, the Russians ordered the cutting of the grid carrying electricity supplies from the central electricity generator in their sector to the Western Sectors of Berlin, and at six o'clock the next morning they also severed all road and barge traffic to and from the city, at the same time halting all supplies — including coal, food and fresh milk — which were drawn from the Soviet Sector. On 24 June, Marshal Sokolovsky announced that the *Komman-datura* had ceased to exist for all practical purposes. There was no longer any doubt: Berlin was under seige.

Only one route remained open, via the three air corridors, but the resources available to implement an airlift operation to relieve Berlin were woefully slender. The Americans had only 100 C-47 transport aircraft in Europe at the time, to which the RAF could add about 150, mostly Dakotas but with a few four-engined Avro Yorks. All this meant that against Berlin's daily food requirement of 13,500 tons, the USAF and RAF between them could probably manage 700 tons at the outside.

The situation was clearly intolerable, and one that prompted US President Harry S. Truman's close advisers to urge caution when it came to talk about an Allied stand over Berlin. Some of the US Army chiefs were cautious, too; among them were Major General William Draper, Under Secretary of the Army, and Lieutenant General Albert Wedemeyer, the Army General Staff's Director of Plans and Operations, who flew to London at short notice on 24 June to sound out the opinion of the British Government. Their surprise was considerable when Ernest Bevin, the Secretary of State for Foreign Affairs, informed them that Prime Minister Clement Attlee's Cabinet had voted not to sanction a withdrawal from Berlin, and that RAF transport aircraft were already flying in supplies. The British Government's viewpoint was that the situation would be back to normal in a few days, once the Russians had made their gesture; nevertheless, the British attitude did much to strengthen American resolve.

British Prime Minister Clement Attlee (left) and Foreign Minister Ernest Bevin acted quickly to get the British air supply operation into action. The speed with which the British Government reacted to the Berlin crisis surprised the Americans.

In Washington, the resolve of President Truman needed no strengthening. He was adamant that the Western Allies should maintain their presence in Berlin, come what may. The real problem was to find a way of keeping them there in the face of mounting Soviet pressure. Truman's instruction to James Forrestal, Secretary of Defense, Kenneth Royall, Secretary of the Army, and Robert Lovett, Under Secretary of State, at a meeting on 25 June left no room for doubt; all resources were to be channelled into forming a viable airlift organization. General LeMay's shoestring air bridge would soon be a thing of the past.

Meanwhile, on 22 June, HQ British Air Forces of Occupation, concerned that the Russians might attempt to interfere with British aircraft flying into Berlin, had ordered eight Hawker Tempest Mk V fighter-bombers of No 80 Squadron to deploy to Gatow to provide escorts for RAF transport aircraft over the Soviet Zone if necessary. They remained until 14 July, when they flew out to Gutersloh in the British Zone. By that time, it had become apparent that the Russians were not going to use force against the Airlift, and in any case the presence of the Tempests at Gatow added to the general congestion.

Chapter Three
Operation 'Plainfare': The RAF Airlift, June-December 1948

When the Russians severed all road and rail links between Berlin and the West on 24 June, Royal Air Force Transport Command had a single squadron of Dakotas in Germany. This was No 30, commanded by Squadron Leader A.M. Johnstone. Having operated as a fighter squadron in the Far East during the Second World War, No 30 had disbanded in December 1946 and re-formed as a transport unit with Dakota C IV aircraft at Oakington, Cambridgeshire, in November 1947.

In May 1948, No 30 Squadron deployed to Schleswigland, on the Baltic coast of Germany, in support of the 16th Independent Parachute Brigade, which had just been withdrawn from Palestine. Schleswigland had originally been opened in 1936 as a civil glider airfield, but had been taken over by the Luftwaffe in 1938. During the war it had been a night-fighter base, with Messerschmitt Me 110s, Junkers Ju 88s and Focke-Wulf Fw 190s; later, it had been allocated to VIP use, with Junkers Ju 52s and '252s operating shuttle services to various points in the dwindling Reich territory, and in the last weeks of the conflict it had been used by Me 262 jet fighters. The Royal Air Force Regiment occupied the field in May 1945, and it was later used by No 121 Fighter Wing until the end of 1946. A few months later it was reopened as an Airborne Forces practice camp, which was still its role in June 1948. By a coincidence, No 30 Squadron's detachment to Schleswigland ended on 25 June, when Johnstone led his nine Dakotas back to Oakington. But they were not to remain in Cambridgeshire for long; a great deal had been happening in their absence.

In May 1948, preliminary orders were issued by HQ No 46 Group to RAF Waterbeach, also in Cambridgeshire, to the effect that one of the Waterbeach Wing's three Dakota squadrons was to stand by to supply the British garrison in Berlin, should this move prove necessary. This commitment was increased to two squadrons in mid-June, and supply plans were drawn up under the code-name of Operation 'Knicker'.

In the evening of 24 June, further orders were received at Waterbeach from HQ No 46 Group that one squadron, comprising eight Dakotas and their crews, was to deploy to Wunstorf and be ready to commence operations to Berlin within 48 hours. The party, under the command of Wing Commander G.H. Gatheral, left between 13:00 and 14:00 local time the next day and began operating that same evening. At midnight on 27/28 June the second detachment of eight Dakotas earmarked for Operation 'Knicker' were also ordered to fly to Wunstorf as soon as possible. They left between 10:45 and 11:30 local time on 28 June.

The original requirement for Operation 'Knicker', as given in No 46 Group Operation Order No 7/48 dated 19 June 1948, was a daily lift of 130,000 lb (58,967 kg) for the maintenance of the British forces in Berlin. This lift required 24 Dakota sorties daily, and was expected to continue for at least a month. Within 48 hours, however, it became apparent that two squadrons of Dakotas would not be enough to sustain what was fast becoming a major effort. Accordingly, a conference was called by the AOC No 46 Group, Air Commodore J.W.F. Merer, of all station commanders and officers command-ing the technical wings at Waterbeach, Oakington and Bassingbourn at 21:00 hours on 28 June. Merer left his subordinates in no doubt that a much larger effort had to be prepared, and that Nos 38 and 47 Groups would also be required to take part in the operation. The greatly enlarged effort was to receive the new code-name of 'Carter Paterson' — a somewhat unfortunate choice, because Carter Paterson were a well-known firm of removal specialists, and removals were not what this operation was all about. So, early in July, 'Carter Paterson' became Operation 'Plainfare'.

The 38 additional aircraft needed for the enlarged airlift flew into Oakington on the morning of 29 June, and positioned at Wunstorf the next day. At the same time, Group Captain Noel Hyde was sent out to Germany by HQ Transport Command to co-ordinate matters. As his subsequent report shows, all was not plain sailing.

'I received instructions on the evening of 29 June from the AOC 46 Group that I was to take over command of transport forces operating in Germany as soon as possible. I reported to Group HQ the next morning to obtain my directive and then flew to Wunstorf, arriving there in the evening. After some confusion over the chain of command [Group Captain Wally Biggar had arrived at Wunstorf from Schleswigland in the interim, having received from the British Air Forces of Occupation exactly the same authority as Hyde] on 3 July AHQ issued Operations Instruction No 14/48, which completely reversed the statements made by the C-in-C and SASO on the two previous days [to the effect that Hyde was going to be in command at Wunstorf]. Para 9 of this Instruction states that BAFO Advanced Headquarters has been formed at RAF Station Wunstorf, and that the officer commanding this headquarters is to exercise operational control over the transport forces allotted to him by AHQ BAFO. This he will do through the Officer Commanding RAF Station Wunstorf, who will in turn exercise control through the Officer Commanding the RAF Transport Wing located at Wunstorf.'

It was an unfortunate start because — although the administration was eventually sorted out — it caused a degree of acrimony between senior officers of Transport Command and BAFO. However, there was no disputing the fact that BAFO was a tactical organization, born out of the wartime RAF 2nd

Tactical Air Force, and that it had no experience in mounting complex transport operations. This task logically fell to No 46 Group, which eventually assumed control of the British Airlift operation.

Wunstorf was not a large airfield. It was originally built in 1934 as part of Hitler's military airfield expansion scheme; by 1939 a Luftwaffe bomber group had been formed there, and this continued to operate throughout 1940. From 1941 until the end of the war the base was occupied mainly in training the crews of twin-engined fighters, although single-engined fighters were dispersed there in the later stages. In May 1945 Wunstorf was occupied by No 123 RAF Fighter-Bomber Wing, which continued to operate from there until the beginning of the Airlift.

By the beginning of July Wunstorf was already heavily congested, with 48 Dakotas of No 30 Squadron (which Squadron Leader Johnstone had been ordered to fly back from Oakington within hours of his return to the UK) plus Nos 46, 53, 77 and 238 Squadrons flying on the Berlin run, together with some aircraft of No 240 Operational Conversion Unit. When Operation 'Plainfare' began, the airfield possessed two concrete runways, perimeter tracks and ladder-type hardstandings. Apart from these, and the aprons in front of the hangars, the surface was grass.

The original Airlift requirement from Wunstorf, as given by No 46 Group Operation Order 9/48 dated 30 June, was for 161 Dakota sorties per day, lifting 400 tons, plus six sorties per day flown by scheduled RAF Dakota services to Berlin, lasting until 3 July. This was to be followed by 84 Dakota sorties lifting 210 tons daily, together with the six sorties required by the personnel services in Berlin, to run from 4 July until further notice. At the same time, No 47 Group was to provide forty Avro York aircraft to fly 120 sorties during this period.

The first twelve Yorks arrived at Wunstorf on the evening of 12 July under Wing Commander G.F.A. Skelton. Owing to the state of the airfield's surface, however, it was decided that only twenty Yorks could be accommodated, at least for the next few days. AHQ were requested to postpone the arrival of the remainder of the force until several ditches had been filled in and some of the parking area covered with PSP (Pierced Steel Planking).

During the first two days of July the lack of adequate surfacing at Wunstorf caused a great many problems, heavy rain and the constant movement of aircraft and vehicles churning up the soil into ankle-deep mud. However, work on the laying of PSP progressed rapidly, enabling the first York reinforcement aircraft to be flown in on 4 and 5 July.

Strict air traffic control procedures were developed for the aircraft plying the route between Wunstorf and the Berlin terminal airfield, Gatow. Taking off on the primary runway — 09 — the transports had to climb straight ahead for two minutes at 145 knots, keeping below 1,000 ft (305 m) before turning port for Walsrode. A take-off on any other runway involved a climb straight ahead for two minutes, and then a turn the shortest way for Walsrode. Height en route was 3,500 ft (1,067 m), and airspeed 160 knots. The outbound route was then

Kitbags packed with supplies being off-loaded from a Dakota at Gatow.

base to Walsrode (26 nm, 013 degrees true); Walsrode to Egestorf (27 nm, 040 degrees true); Egestorf to Restorf (52 nm, 102 degrees true); and finally Restorf to Frohnau (69 nm, 110 degrees true).

On arrival at the twenty-mile (32 km) check point from Frohnau Beacon, aircraft were to make their initial call on Gatow Airways, passing call-sign, height, ETA Frohnau and the type of load carried. On receipt of this call, Gatow Airways provided QNH (altimeter setting above sea level), airfield elevation, runway in use, surface wind speed and direction, and also cleared the aircraft to descend to its allocated height at the Frohnau Beacon. On reaching the latter, the aircraft captain changed to the QNH altimeter setting and called Gatow Approach for his clearance. A GCA was the primary and standard approach method, and was used regardless of weather conditions.

In the case of a westerly landing, after contacting Gatow Approach at Frohnau the aircraft turned on to a heading of 180 degrees Magnetic and homed on to the Grunewald Beacon, descending to 1,500 ft (457 m). Aircraft were instructed not to descend below 2,000 ft (609 m) until south of Tegel. At Grunewald Beacon, the aircraft turned on to a new heading of 260 degrees Magnetic and changed frequency to the final controller for the final approach and landing. Immediately the pilot made visual contact with the field, he changed frequency to Gatow Tower for completion of the landing.

For an easterly landing, after contacting Gatow Approach at Frohnau aircraft turned on to a heading of 210 degrees Magnetic and homed on to the Huston Beacon, maintaining a height of not less than 2,500 ft (762 m). At Huston Beacon, the aircraft altered course to 260 degrees Magnetic, which was to be held until six miles (9.6 km) downwind of Runway 08, the aircraft descending to 1,500 ft (457 m) in the meantime. At this point, the aircraft turned port on to a heading of 090 degrees Magnetic and changed frequency to the final controller.

On the return flight to Wunstorf, the aircraft flew at 3,500 ft (1,067 m) and an airspeed of 160 knots via Prutzke and Volkenrode back to base. A westerly take-off was the simplest, the aircraft climbing straight out towards Prutzke; in the case of an easterly take-off, the aircraft turned starboard, homing on the Wannsee Beacon, which was crossed at 1,500 ft (457 m) before climbing to route height towards Prutzke.

On 5 July, Air Commodore Merer visited the Transport Command detachment at Wunstorf and said that more flying hours could be supported than the total originally planned. It was estimated that 112 sorties per day could be sustained until 31 July. On 16 July, a signal was received from HQ 46 Group to the effect that the Dakotas were exceeding the flying hours that could be supported, so the daily rate was reduced to 102 sorties. This was followed, the next day, by a signal from HQ Transport Command permitting the Dakotas to fly 2,000 hours during the next seven days and 1,700 hours per week subsequently. The daily rate was increased to 125 sorties. This signal superseded an earlier one from No 46 Group, which had restricted the daily sortie rate by the Dakotas to 92.

No difficulty was experienced in completing the Operation 'Knicker' task up to 29 June. In fact, the planned lift of 130,000 lb (58,968 kg) was exceeded by almost 30,000 lb (13,608 kg), without any increase in the planned number of sorties. This was achieved by the removal of unnecessary items of safety equipment such as dinghies.

During the first phase of Operation 'Plainfare' — 30 June to 3 July — the target of 160 sorties per day was not reached. The primary cause of this was bad weather, with rain and low cloud seriously affecting the flow of aircraft. The cloud was often down to below 200 ft (61 m), and GCA was in almost continuous use. Minor unserviceability also compounded the problem. Most often, this was caused by dampness affecting the electrical equipment. At the beginning, there was also a shortage of all kinds of ground equipment, ranging from petrol bowsers to starter trolleys and chocks. Occasional holdups were created, too, by loading difficulties resulting from a lack of manpower.

During the second phase of Operation 'Plainfare', which ran from 4 to 19 July, the addition of No 47 Group's Avro Yorks rapidly increased the daily lift, which rose from 474 tons on 6 July to 995 tons on 18 July. The lift would have been greater, had it not been for several factors. Firstly, the bad weather continued throughout the whole of this period, causing flying to be halted or at best slowed down on many occasions. The Air Traffic Control at Gatow frequently stopped all flying, or alternatively refused to accept aircraft at intervals of less than fifteen minutes. The airfield surface became very badly cut up by MT, with the result that a number of aircraft became bogged. Secondly, the Avro Yorks had serviceability problems. It had been planned originally for

Avro Yorks of No 51 Squadron on the tarmac at Gatow in July 1948. The hangar in the foreground is stacked with sacks of mail.

the Yorks to fly 120 sorties a day, but at no time during this period did they exceed 100 sorties. In fact, the daily average was 77. Because of the state of the airfield, only half the York force of forty aircraft could be accepted before 4-5 July.

With the arrival of the 47 Group detachment, a central Force Headquarters was formed to co-ordinate the activities and requirements of both the Dakota and York elements. The organization worked well, although to begin with there was a natural tendency for direct communications between Group elements and their parent Groups without reference to Force HQ. This occasionally led to small misunderstandings and some duplication.

All crews were pooled, and some consequently had to lose their identity — an unavoidable move which caused some grumbles. In the Dakota detachment there were elements of nine squadrons, Nos 18, 27, 30, 46, 53, 62, 77, 113 and 238, the latter being re-numbered No 10 Squadron in November 1948. These were drawn in the main from RAF Waterbeach (Nos 18, 53 and 62) and RAF Oakington (Nos 27, 30 and 46), although No 77 came from Broadwell, No 113 from Fairford and No 238 from Abingdon. The bulk of No 47 Group's York force was also drawn from Abingdon, which provided aircraft from Nos 40, 59 and 242 squadrons; other Yorks were provided by Nos 206 and 511 Squadrons at Lyneham, and by No 51 Squadron at Bassingbourn.

Before the Yorks began operating, the Dakotas were spaced at six-minute intervals by day and fifteen-minute intervals by night. These rates were found

Avro Yorks of No 242 Squadron at RAF Lyneham after taking part in the Berlin Airlift.

to be the fastest that the servicing and loading parties could maintain, although later, when more experience had been accumulated and additional equipment and ground personnel were available, a faster flow was possible. When the Yorks started to operate, a fresh problem arose because of the difference in speed between the York and Dakota. The outward and return routes between Wunstorf and Gatow were spaced as widely apart as the corridor allowed, and the different types of aircraft were separated in height, but there was a risk of collision while climbing to and descending from the operating altitudes. Experience showed that it was difficult for aircraft to take off at definite pre-determined times, so the flying programme was divided into waves of each type of aircraft, timed so that the last Dakota of one wave was not overtaken by the first York of the next, and so that the last York would be leaving the unloading point at Gatow as the first Dakota arrived.

The system worked well except that it created an uneven flow of work for the ground crews, so a new system was devised whereby the two types of aircraft were phased in at their best hourly rate, the flow being timed so that all aircraft, regardless of type, arrived at Gatow at four-minute intervals. When the rate of flow of aircraft into Gatow had to be reduced because of weather conditions, the York sorties were maintained while the Dakota sorties were reduced or cancelled, a move designed to take advantage of the York's greater load capacity. This resulted in the loss of considerable Dakota effort, and the Dakota crews, although appreciating why this action was necessary, felt somewhat irritated by it.

Great difficulty was experienced in getting aircraft off at a fixed time, the reason being that, unlike most operations in which ample time was available in which to prepare aircraft, on 'Plainfare' aircraft had to be serviced in the quickest possible time. The result was that crews would often arrive at their aircraft only to find that some small snag in loading or servicing was causing a delay. Such delays caused the whole programme to become disorganized, and take-off times tended to degenerate into a free-for-all, with a resulting uneven traffic flow that increased the risk of collision and made unloading, loading and servicing still more difficult.

To overcome this, a system of starting clearance was introduced. Air Traffic Control were given a complete list of the day's sorties, showing the type of aircraft involved and the time of take-off for each sortie. Captains were instructed to call flying control by R/T when their aircraft were completely ready, and ask for starting clearance. ATC then looked up the next vacant slot for that particular type of aircraft, and providing there was sufficient time for the aircraft to be started up and taxied to the runway, gave permission to start and time to take off. If for any reason an aircraft was not ready for a particular sortie, that sortie was automatically cancelled. This system was introduced on 15 July 1948, but was later discontinued at the request of the Station Commander because of the extra work it imposed on ATC. However, it worked very smoothly while it was in operation, most aircraft getting away on time.

A considerable amount of minor unserviceability was experienced. On 3 July, at one time, there were 22 aircraft unserviceable, mostly with electrical trouble aggravated by the damp conditions. In the main, this minor unserviceability problem was due to the short duration of flights and the rapid turn-round required.

At the beginning of the operation, the Dakotas operated with a maximum landing weight of 27,000 lb (12,247 kg), giving a payload of 5,500 lb (2,495 kg). This payload was increased to 6,500 lb (2,948 kg) by removing all unnecessary items of safety equipment and by a reduction in the petrol load. On 16 July, authority was received from HQ Transport Command for the Dakota take-off and landing weights to be increased to 28,750 lb and 28,000 lb (13,041 and 12,700 kg) respectively, giving a payload of 7,500 lb (3,402 kg).

It was originally estimated that the Dakotas would require thirty minutes for turning round at base, but in practice it was found that 45 minutes were needed, mainly because of the distance between the aircraft's parking position, load control, and the hangar. The possibility of introducing central loading and refuelling points was considered, but owing to the lack of suitable hard standings, congestion on the airfield and the blockage liable to be caused by an unserviceable aircraft, the scheme was not introduced. At Gatow, where no refuelling took place, turn-round time from landing to take-off averaged twenty minutes.

It was planned that, of the forty Yorks available, thirty should be operating at any one time, flying a daily total of 120 sorties. However, this was found to

Above *Loading a Dakota C IV with tyres at No 1 Transport Aircraft Maintenance Unit, RAF Honington. No 1 TAMU was responsible for providing spares for the RAF Dakota fleet in Germany throughout the Airlift.*

Below *In July 1948 the RAF Central Bomber Establishment carried out experiments in dropping sacks of coal from Lincolns in case this proved necessary to supply Berlin. In the event, it did not. This photograph shows coal sacks being loaded into a Lincoln's bomb bay.*

be impracticable, due to unserviceability, and it was eventually agreed that 100 sorties per day was the maximum that could reasonably be expected. Again, as with the Dakotas, the Yorks' unserviceability was due mainly to short flights, averaging one hour's duration; this was certain to produce many minor snags in an aircraft designed for long-range operations. In addition, the frequent landings made with a full load imposed a heavy strain on tyres and brakes. Apart from this, the Yorks were not established for continual daily servicing, most of this being carried out at RAF staging posts during normal operations, and this remained a problem until No 47 Group sent out extra ground personnel to Germany.

To begin with, the Yorks were operated at a maximum loaded wieght of 60,000 lb (27,216 kg). On 16 July their landing weight was increased to 65,000 lb (29,484 kg) on receipt of the HQ Transport Command authority, and the maximum take-off weight went up to 67,000 lb (30,391 kg). This gave a payload of 16,500 lb (7,484 kg) for the York freighter, and 15,000 lb (6,804 kg) for the passenger-freighter. Difficulty was experienced in loading the passenger-freighter version because of the size of the door and its position under the wing.

The original estimate for the turn-round time for York aircraft at base was two hours, but after a few days of operations it was found that two and a half hours was the average time required. The average time spent on the ground by the Yorks at Gatow was 40-45 minutes.

Communications were bad, although the Royal Corps of Signals went to great efforts to provide and maintain the necessary telephones and land-lines. Telephone calls to HQ took a very long time to get through, and the quality of

Blockade or not, some Service children reached Berlin in the summer of 1948 to spend their holidays with their parents. This group of twenty children travelled via the Hook of Holland and flew from Bückeburg to Gatow.

Sunderland GR5 of No 201 Squadron loading stores on Berlin's Havel See prior to the return flight to Finkenwerder, on the Elbe.

speech was poor. The lines to the UK were sometimes so bad that the call had to be abandoned.

On 19 July, the small Transport Wing HQ formed at Wunstorf at the start of 'Carter Paterson' was disbanded and replaced by a Transport Operations section in an operations room at the Schloss at Bückeburg, Headquarters of the British Air Forces of Occupation. The official brief of this section was to 'co-ordinate air transport operations as far as possible with Army and Control Commission Germany requirements', which really meant that 'Plainfare' operations were now under the control of BAFO. However, the detailed conduct of the Airlift was delegated to the Station Commander, Wunstorf.

When Operation 'Knicker' was planned, it was imagined that two RAF air movements sections would be capable of handling the limited amount of freight and passengers to be airlifted each day. However, the magnitude and scope of the task involved in the greatly enlarged Operation 'Carter Paterson' (subsequently 'Plainfare') proved to be far beyond the capacity of the RAF air movements organization, and on 28 June an HQ Army Air Transport Organization (AATO) was formed by HQ British Army of the Rhine at Wunstorf alongside the Transport Wing HQ, with a Rear Airfield Supply Organization (RASO) at Wunstorf and a Forward Airfield Supply Organization (FASO) at Gatow. The HQ AATO was later transferred to the Schloss at Bückeburg, where it worked alongside the transport operations room — and later alongside HQ No 46 Group when the latter arrrived in Germany in September to assume executive control of the Airlift operations.

Meanwhile, on 5 July, the transport force had been augmented by ten Short Sunderland flying-boats of Nos 201 and 230 Squadrons from RAF Calshot. These aircraft operated a shuttle service from a temporary base at Finkenwerder, on the River Elbe west of Hamburg, to the Havel See (Lake Havel) adjoining Gatow airfield, each aircraft carrying 4½ tons of supplies into Berlin and bringing out manufactured goods and undernourished refugees on each trip. By good organization, using DUKW amphibious vehicles for unloading, the turn-round times were reduced to twenty minutes at Hamburg and twelve minutes at Berlin. In spite of frequent fog and danger from floating debris, the Sunderlands made over 1,000 sorties, carrying in 4,500 tons of food and bringing out 1,113 starving children, until ice-flows on the Havel See brought flying-boat operations to a halt on 15 December. The Sunderlands (and two civilian Short Hythe flying-boats) were the only aircraft used on the Airlift whose internal anti-corrosion treatment, a necessary protection against salt water, permitted them to carry bulk salt, which was urgently needed in West Berlin since supplies from Staasfürt had been cut off. The two Sunderland GR 5 squadrons together formed No 235 Operational Conversion Unit under the command of Wing Commander (later Group Captain) D.B. Fitzpatrick, OBE, AFC.

The Sunderland operations were handicapped throughout by the lack of adequate ground navigation and landing approach aids; there had also been some difficulty in phasing them into the Berlin air traffic pattern. No such problems were experienced when the first civilian charter operator began flying from Bückeburg to Gatow on 27 July (see Chapter Six, The civil airlift).

By the middle of July the concentration of Dakotas, Yorks and civil aircraft resulting from the rapid build-up of the transport force far exceeded the capacity of Wunstorf to operate the aircraft efficiently and to accommodate the personnel. Accordingly, on 29 July the RAF and civil Dakotas were moved to Fassberg, the four-engined civil types remaining at Wunstorf with the RAF Yorks. Fassberg had originally been completed in 1936 as the base for a Luftwaffe bombing school, but during the war it became a technical training station until the later months, when it was used by operational squadrons as the Luftwaffe retreated before the advancing Allied forces. After the war, until December 1947, Fassberg was used for a time as an RAF fighter base, but was subsequently reduced to a care and maintenance basis. The expansion of the airfield to meet the needs of Operation 'Plainfare' consequently involved a large programme of works services; these included the complete renovation of twelve barrack blocks and the former technical school, the conversion of two hangar annexes and two office buildings into domestic accommodation, the clearance of some five acres (two hectares) of forest, and the laying of about 180,000 sq yd (150,498 m²) of PSP hardstanding and five miles (8 km) of railway sidings.

Group Captain Biggar, who was responsible for overseeing the work that was to turn Fassberg into an operational 'Plainfare' base, knew exactly what his priority was. Work began immediately on the hardstanding, which measured 800 by 500 yd (731 by 457 m) and it was ready for use by the Dakotas in just seven days.

The Dakotas stayed there until 22 August, when Fassberg was handed over to the USAF and forty USAF C-54s moved in and the RAF aircraft, plus the civil Dakotas, were transferred to Lübeck, yet another airfield built in 1935

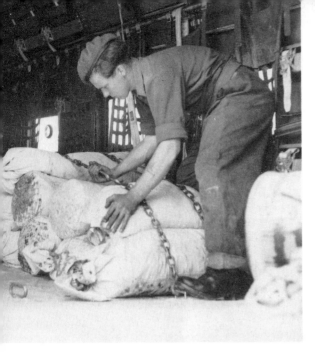

Left *Driver Cox of the RASC securing Service kitbags aboard a Dakota about to leave Fassberg for Berlin in the early weeks of the Airlift.*

Below *Unlike USAF C-47s which were replaced by C-54s, the RAF's Dakotas soldiered on until the end of the Airlift. This photograph shows spares being loaded into KN274 at Lübeck.*

Right *Unloading sacks of coal from a Dakota at Gatow.*

under the Luftwaffe's expansion scheme. During the early part of the war it was used by Heinkel He 111 bombers, then it became a fighter training station, and during the latter part of the war Junkers Ju 88 night fighters were based there. After the war the airfield became an Armament Practice Camp for the fighter squadrons of BAFO and Fighter Command.

As had been the case at Fassberg, the expansion necessary for Lübeck use as

a 'Plainfare' base was extensive, involving an extension to the existing concrete runway, the laying of PSP hardstandings and a parking apron about 88,000 sq yd (73,576 m²) in area. In addition, the railhead capacity was doubled by laying additional spurs. Fortunately, the former Luftwaffe airfields were already well served with these; more than one senior RAF officer looked wistfully upon the rail links and wished that RAF airfields were similarly equipped. Other major works services included the laying of a concrete road to the petrol bulk installations about 4,000 sq yd (3,344 m²) in area, horizontal bar and centreline approach lighting and high-intensity runway lighting, and lighting for the loading and unloading areas.

Operating from Lübeck needed special care, for the eastern boundary of the airfield lay only two miles (3.2 km) from the edge of the Soviet Zone, and an instrument approach from that direction involved flying over Russian territory. The normal take-off procedures from Lübeck were as follows:

Take-off on Runway 26: Climb straight ahead to 400 ft (122 m) at 110 knots, do a climbing turn to starboard on to 340 degrees Magnetic, hold this course for one minute, then do a climbing turn to starboard to set course over Base Eureka (the ground equipment associated with the Rebecca receiver carried in the aircraft) at 2,000 ft (609 m).

Take-off on Runway 08: Climb straight ahead to 400 ft (122 m) at 110 knots, do a climbing turn to port on to Magnetic North, climb on this course for one minute, and then a climbing turn to port on to 180 degrees Magnetic to set course over Base Eureka at 2,000 ft (609 m).

Outbound to Gatow, the Dakotas maintained a height of 5,500 ft (1,676 m) and an airspeed of 125 knots. The route was base to 53°30' North, 10°45' East (eighteen nautical miles on a heading of 177 degrees true), from there to Restorf (38 nm, 137 degrees true), and Restorf to Frohnau (69 nm, 110 degrees true.)

Inbound from Gatow the Dakotas also maintained 5,500 ft (1,676 m), but at an increased speed of 135 knots and, of course, following a different route: Gatow to Ruhen (82 nm, 271 degrees true); Ruhen to Luneburg (49 nm, 343 degrees true); Luneburg to Tremsbüttel (29 nm, 348 degrees true); and finally the sixteen nautical mile leg from Tremsbüttel to base on 174 degrees true.

The freight carried from Lübeck included coal, newsprint and a considerable amount of German economic cargo. With elements of seven RAF Dakota squadrons (Nos 18, 27, 30, 46, 62 and 77 Squadrons) now operating out of Lübeck, together with eighteen civil Dakotas belonging to Air Contractors, Air Transport, British Nederland Air Services, BOAC, Ciros Aviation, Hornton Airways, Kearsley Airways, Scottish Airlines, Sivewright Airways, Trent Valley Aviation and Westminster Airways, congestion at the airfield was reaching a critical level, so on 5 October all civil Dakotas were transferred to Fühlsbüttel, the civil airport of Hamburg which was controlled by the Civil Aviation Control Commission of Germany.

The transfer of these aircraft created an unusual situation, even in Airlift terms. Hitherto, all aircraft belonging to the civilian charter companies had been located at RAF stations; their operations had been co-ordinated with those of the RAF squadrons by the Station Commander, and the RAF had also accommodated their crews, as well as providing a number of other essential services. Now, although their operations continued to be directed and controlled by the RAF, and an Army RASO was provided for the loading and documenting of aircraft, the responsibility for providing the services previously supplied by the RAF now fell to the Control Commission of Germany, the executive authority at Fühlsbüttel being the Airport Manager. However, RAF operations officers were attached to the civilian operations staff at the airport for briefing and control purposes.

In mid-September, the RAF Dakota force at Lübeck was augmented by the arrival of twelve Dakota crews of No 1 (Dominion) Squadron, Royal Australian Air Force. In October, ten crews of No 2 (Dominion) Squadron South African Air Force also arrived, followed by three Royal New Zealand Air Force crews in November. The RNZAF men were attached to the Australians. All the Commonwealth crews flew the RAF Dakotas and operated continuously up to the end of the Airlift as part of the Dakota force, making an extremely valuable contribution to the success of Operation 'Plainfare'.

The high intensity of the operations during the first three months of 'Plainfare' inevitably produced their crop of accidents — only one of which, fortunately, had fatal results. The first occurred on 21 July, when Dakota KN641, en route to the United Kingdom for servicing, suffered engine failure and had to make a forced landing at Schipol; the next day, a similar failure forced Dakota KN213 into making an emergency landing at Gatow. Then, on 26 July, Dakota KN252 caught fire in the air and crashed near Fassberg, fortunately without loss of life. On 28 July York MW315 was damaged in an unloading accident at Gatow, and on 3 August there were three separate incidents, two involving Dakotas and one a York. At Bückeburg, Dakota KN507 sustained damage when it swung off the runway, while Dakota KN238 suffered severe damage when an engine caught fire shortly before landing at Gatow. The accident to the York, MW199, occurred at Wunstorf when the driver of a fuel bowser struck the trailing edge of the aircraft's wing. Two Dakotas, KN631 and KN355, were damaged in accidents on the ground at Lübeck on 17 and 18 September. Then, on 19 September, York MW288 crashed at Wunstorf after suffering engine failure during a night take-off. All five crew (Flight Lieutenants H.W. Thomson and G. Kell, Navigator L.E.H. Gilbert, Signaller 2 S.M.L. Towersey and Engineer 2 E.W. Watson) were killed. Nor was this all: the accidents listed above involved only aircraft that needed to be salvaged as a result, this work being carried out by No 1 Salvage Detachment at Luneburg. There was a spate of lesser accidents involving damage that could be made good on the spot.

Meanwhile, in August RAF Transport Command had found itself with a major problem. The progressive build-up of the RAF transport force in Germany since the beginning of 'Plainfare' had only been accomplished by the withdrawal of aircraft and crews from the strategic air routes and from the Transport Command training organization, which had been completely skeletonized. It now became apparent that unless the training programme was resumed, at least in part, the normal wastage of aircrews on 'Plainfare' could not be made good. The decision was therefore made to recommence training within Transport Command at about 75 per cent of the former capacity, and by the end of September ten Yorks and twenty Dakotas, with 36 instructor aircrews, had been withdrawn from the operation. The decision was inevitable under the circumstances, but the effect was a significant drop in the daily tonnage lifted by the RAF into Berlin — a deficiency that would not be made good until the arrival of the first Handley Page Hastings transports at Schleswigland in November.

About the end of August, there were indications that the Russians might be prepared to discuss the political situation in Berlin, the inference being that the surface communications between the city and the Allied Zones of Germany might soon be restored. The indications proved false, and it now became evident that the Airlift must not only be maintained at its existing capacity, but that it would have to be greatly expanded during the winter months ahead.

By this date, the transport force, including RAF, USAF and British civil aircraft operating from the British Zone into Gatow and the Havel Lake, was located at four bases — Wunstorf, Fassberg, Lübeck and Finkenwerder. The control of their operations, and in particular the co-ordination of the traffic within the corridors and in the local Berlin area, could no longer be handled effectively by the operations staff at HQ BAFO and the transport operations room at Bückeburg. Weaknesses in the co-ordination of aircraft servicing, loading and despatching at individual bases, and the lack of a standardized system of operational control, added to the difficulty. Moreover, the air and ground crews were beginning to feel the strain of a highly intensive and prolonged routine which had developed on the supposition that the operation would only last for a few weeks. The overall stress was heightened by long flying

General William H. Tunner, the very able and experienced commander of the Combined Airlift Task Force.

and working hours, and by overcrowded domestic accommodation.

On 22 September, an advanced operational headquarters of HQ No 46 Group was detached from Transport Command to Germany. Its task was to take over executive control of all operations involving British aircraft on the Airlift under the orders of the AOC-in-C BAFO. This 'Advanced Headquarters, No 46 Group' comprised a skeleton air staff — including signals, navigation, air movements and aircraft control — and technical staff with a small administrative liaison element, the whole numbering thirteen officers and eight airmen. The AHQ was located in the Schloss, Bückeburg, alongside HQ AATO, and absorbed the transport operations room already there.

On 15 October 1948, discussions between HQ BAFO and HQ USAFE resulted in the establishment of a Combined Airlift Task Force (CALTF) at Wiesbaden. Its commander was Major-General William H. Tunner, USAF, who during the war had been in charge of the airlift task force engaged in flying supplies from India to China over the 'Hump'. The freight lifted over the Himalayas during that operation had reached 71,000 tons per month, a total that was to be almost quadrupled during the Berlin Airlift. Tunner's deputy was Air Commodore Merer, the AOC No 46 Group, who remained at Bückeburg with his headquarters.

On 1 November 1948, the RAF's contribution to the Berlin Airlift received a considerable boost with the arrival at Schleswigland of the first Hastings C Mk 1 aircraft of No 47 Squadron from RAF Dishforth, in Yorkshire. Powered by four Bristol Hercules radial engines, the Hastings could carry an eight-ton payload at a cruising speed of a little over 300 mph (483 km/h). No 47

Squadron began operations to Berlin, initially with eight aircraft, on 11 November; a month later it was joined by No 297 Squadron, also equipped with Hastings and from Dishforth. The third Hastings squadron to take part in the Airlift was No 53, but this did not begin to re-equip with the four-engined transports until August 1949, and so was involved only in the run-down of Operation 'Plainfare'.

Schleswigland was soon a thriving centre of operations for both the RAF Hastings and the Halton tankers of the Lancashire Aircraft Company. The crews of both were grateful for one thing: because a considerable time had elapsed between the decision to bring the station into use and the date when flying commenced, the majority of the building improvements had been completed before the aircraft arrived. Work included the construction of an additional hangar, the building of a large apron to increase the area of the eastern hardstandings, the extension of a rail spur to the RASO area on the east side of the field, and the enlargement of aviation fuel storage installations.

On 15 December 1948 Tegel, Berlin's third airfield, was formally opened for Airlift traffic. This airfield, which was situated in the French Sector of Berlin, did not exist prior to the Airlift. The completely new base was built solely to accommodate part of the overload of traffic burdening Tempelhof and Gatow. Laid out on an area which had previously been earmarked as the most suitable place for the delivery of supplies by parachute, Tegel was ready for operation just four months after the first ground was broken in August.

The building operations at Tegel were conducted by the Americans and carried out with German labour, much of it female. In fact, forty per cent of the 17,000 civilian employees were women. They worked around the clock for DM 1.20 per hour, plus a hot meal every shift — very viable currency in Berlin in those times. A single runway, 5,500 ft long and 150 ft wide (1,676 by 46 m), was built of a 22 in (56 cm) thickness of tightly packed brick rubble and crushed rock taken from bombed buildings and penetrated with an asphalt binding. The Americans also took ballast from disused railway tracks, a technique much used in Germany by British engineers. In similar fashion, aprons totalling 120,000 sq ft (11,148 m²) and 6,020 lineal feet (1,835 m) of taxiways, varying from 50 ft to 120 ft (15 to 36 m) in width, were constructed. The new base also required access roads of 3,200 by 40 and 1,200 by 20 feet (975 by 12 and 366 by 6 m), together with railroads totaling 2,750 ft (838 m). In addition, buildings were erected for administration, operations, the control tower, fire station, infirmary, transportation office and guardhouse, along with a warehouse, a small hangar, adequate hardstandings and many other facilities.

On 18 November 1948, the first aircraft landed at Tegel. It was Dakota KN446 of No 30 Squadron, flown by Squadron Leader A.M. Johnstone, who was making the trip at the request of HQ No 46 Group to find out if the airfield was ready for operation and who brought with him a mixed load of tractor tyres, cooking oil and condensed milk. Johnstone quickly found that the airfield was far from ready; the runway and taxiways were suitable, but the rest of the surface was thick, glutinous mud. Moreover, there seemed to be no system for receiving aircraft, and none at all for offloading cargo. In the end, Johnstone brought his load back to Lübeck in frustration.

When Tegel did open, it was without GCA or BABS (Blind Approach Beacon System), had an airfield control equipped only with VHF, a non-operational control tower, no direct tie-line to the Berlin Air Safety Centre, no facilities for hot meals, no latrines, no water points and no accommodation of any kind. Nevertheless, with the passage of time and the improvement of services Tegel made an enormous difference to the flow of goods to and from Berlin. Incoming freight consisted mainly of coal, liquid fuels and food brought in from Fassberg, Schleswigland and Fühlsbüttel. The handling of cargo and civilian labour was dealt with by the French Air Force, while flying operations were controlled by the USAF.

On 19 November, the day after Squadron Leader Johnstone made the initial flight into Tegel, the Airlift claimed more lives — those of one of his crews. That night, nine of No 30 Squadron's Dakotas — or rather its crews, because the aircraft themselves were pooled — set out from Lübeck to Gatow at the standard five-minute intervals. Johnstone himself was duty operations officer, so he stayed behind. One of the Dakotas sent off was flown by Pilot I. Trezona, the only one of the nine without an instrument rating. However, he had been an instructor on BABS for some eighteen months, and as the Lübeck weather was relatively clear — at least by usual standards — Johnstone had no qualms about letting him take part in this operation, although he took the precaution of putting Trezona in the middle of the block, with four rated pilots ahead of him and four behind.

By the time the Dakotas returned the weather had deteriorated at Lübeck. The cloud base had crept down, although visibility was still about a mile. The first Dakota to return was Trezona's *KN223*, which made a normal BABS approach over the Soviet Zone and called 'finals' at six miles. In the control tower, they waited for Trezona to call when he broke cloud; if he had not done so at 500 ft (152 m), the break-off height for an unrated pilot, he was to abandon his approach, overshoot and divert to Wunstorf. But time passed, and there was no call from Trezona. Several 'overshoot' commands from the controller produced no response from *KN223*. Then the captain of the second Dakota to make its approach, Pilot 2 Pullen, broke cloud and reported that he could see a large fire below him. There was no longer any doubt that *KN223* had gone down in the Russian Zone.

The next day Squadron Leader Johnstone, having failed to secure permission from the Soviet authorities to enter their Zone to search for the missing Dakota, went looking for it from the air. He flew a pattern extending eight miles (13 km) into the Russian Zone from Lübeck and three miles (5 km) either side of the airfield, but neither he nor the volunteer lookouts aboard his Dakota saw anything. Yet the Russians claimed to have found a crashed aircraft, with one badly injured survivor and the remains of three other people in the burnt-out wreckage.

This posed another mystery, because there had been only three in Trezona's crew and the Dakotas had flown out freight, not passengers, from Berlin. Later, however, it was discovered that the fourth person on KN223 was Sergeant P. Dowling, a soldier who had been given compassionate leave. Trezona had been asked to fly him to Lübeck and, although not authorized to carry passengers, had agreed to do so and had taken off immediately — which explained why he had been the first aircraft in the returning wave. The other person killed in the crash was Signaller 3 P.A. Lough; the navigator, Flight Lieutenant J.G. Wilkins, died in hospital in Schöneberg a fortnight later.

On 1 December, the administrative responsibility for the five RAF Airlift stations in the British Zone — Schleswigland, Lübeck, Celle, Fassberg and Wunstorf, together with the Berlin terminal at Gatow — was transferred to the AOC No 46 Group. The situation prior to this was that HQ No 46 Group had exercised operational control of the stations which HQ BAFO administered. A similar arrangement existed at Rhein-Main and Wiesbaden, the two Airlift bases in the American Zone, until a month or two before the end of full-scale Airlift operations, HQ CALTF operating the aircraft while HQ USAFE administered the bases.

On 15 December, Celle was opened as an operational base for a Group of four squadrons of USAF C-54s. Celle had been built in 1935 by the Luftwaffe and used primarily as a training base during the Second World War, although for a time during the Battle of Germany it was occupied by the Junkers 88s of *Behelfs Beleuchter Staffel* 1 (No 1 Illuminator Squadron), which assisted single-engined night fighters in their 'Wild Boar' operations. After the war it was occupied by No 36 Wing RAF and No 84 Group Communication Flight, both of which units remained there until No 1 Barracks Equipment Disposal Unit moved in late 1947.

In mid-September 1948, with Operation 'Plainfare' two and a half months old, the RAF began converting Celle into an Airlift base, employing some 2,000 German workers in the formidable task of constructing the necessary operational facilities and housing. The task of building up Celle to meet Airlift requirements involved the construction of a 5,400 by 150 ft (1,646 by 46 m) runway, a PSP loading apron covering 190,000 sq ft (17,651 m²), and a 9,500 by 50 ft (2,895 by 15 m) PSP taxiway. A great deal of other construction, including houses, rail facilities and a fuel storage complex, was required to develop Celle into a base which, ultimately, was to be considered as a model for Airlift needs.

The decision to develop this second base for USAF C-54s was taken mainly because there was a lack of sites at the entrance to the Frankfurt corridor suitable for development as bases for the additional C-54s which were planned for the Airlift. Also, a far higher utilization of aircraft would result from the shorter distance to be flown to and from Berlin. At the time, consideration had been given to transferring a major part of the C-54 force to the British Zone for this reason, but a study of the weather differential throughout the year between the British and American Zones indicated that it was desirable to maintain half the force in each Zone. Later experience proved the wisdom of this decision, at least in the winter months, since on a number of occasions operations were able to continue uninterrupted in one Zone while adverse weather brought them to a halt in the other.

The command and administrative systems at Fassberg and Celle were similar. Both were RAF stations commanded by RAF officers, although in March 1949 the command of Fassberg was given to a USAF officer. The USAF retained control of their own operations and technical servicing, the latter with the assistance of the RAF Station workshops (see Chapter Four).

On 17 December, 1948, Avro York MW232 (Flight Lieutenant Beeston) airlifted a cargo of canned meat into Gatow. It was the 100,000th ton of provisions brought in by Operation 'Plainfare', and Frau Louise Schroeder, the Deputy Mayor, was at the airfield to receive the incoming York with due ceremony. On 20 December, a Christmas concert was given for German employees at Gatow, and during the next two days special parties were organized at which over 1,000 children were fed and entertained. Sweets and chocolates were distributed among the children as a special treat; many of the little ones did not know what they were, for they had never seen such luxuries before.

On 23 December the 50,000th 'Plainfare' landing was made at Gatow; a further 2,031 landings were made during the week that followed, bringing the total number of sorties during December to 6,737. This was much lower than the totals for November and October, bad weather having taken its toll of the operation, and on 22, 23 and 24 December there were no Dakota flights from Lübeck because of fog. Nevertheless, there was no doubt that Operation 'Plainfare' was succeeding, and for some British Servicemen in Berlin there came the best Christmas present of all; the rescinding of the order which, for six months, had prevented wives and children from joining them. Twelve families had been waiting to go to Berlin when the Russians' action prevented them in June; the backlog was much more considerable now, but Operation 'Union' got under way smoothly and the first families arrived in time for Christmas.

Meanwhile, the French had also given a sort of Christmas present to the Allied pilots landing at Tegel, who had been plagued by the only obstacle in the area; the mast of the Soviet-controlled Berlin Radio transmitter in the French Sector. On 16 December, incoming pilots reported that the mast was no longer there: the French had blown it up. However, there was a kick-back; Major-General Kotikov, the Soviet Commandant, made a personal protest to France's General Ganeval. Under the threat of stronger Soviet action, the French agreed to return the Stolpe district of Berlin to Russian control. It had been allocated to the French as an airfield site, but now that Tegel was in operation they no longer needed it.

Berlin Radio was soon on the air again, broadcasting from a new station at Grunau in the Soviet Zone. There would be plenty of propaganda for it to pour out in 1949, as the Russians came to realize fully that they were losing their stranglehold on the city.

Chapter Four
Operation 'Vittles': The USAF Airlift, June-December 1948

The United States Air Force began its Airlift commitment with one big advantage: it possessed the best-appointed air base in western Germany. Largely destroyed by bombing during the war, Rhein-Main, near Frankfurt, had first been developed by the Germans as a lighter-than-air base for the big commercial airships, the *Graf Zeppelin* and the ill-fated *Hindenburg*. Later, for most of the war, it had become an important Luftwaffe fighter base, and in the closing weeks of the conflict, following the Luftwaffe's withdrawal, it had been occupied by a USAAF P-47 Thunderbolt Group, and after Germany's surrender it was rapidly developed as a vital 'gateway to Europe' for civil aircraft operations, as well as becoming an important USAF sub-command.

At the start of the Berlin crisis, Rhein-Main was used by ten commercial airlines and was the European terminal for the USAF's Military Air Transport Service. Its 'resident' USAF flying unit in June 1948, equipped with C-47s, was the 61st Troop Carrier Group, comprising the 14th, 15th and 53rd Troop Carrier Squadrons. Rhein-Main had a 6,000 by 150 ft (1,829 by 46m) runway, which was to prove adequate for Airlift operations until the spring of 1949, when the tempo of Operation 'Vittles' was stepped up and a new 7,000 by 200 ft (2,133 by 61 m) runway was started. This project, however, was only twenty per cent complete when the Airlift phase-out began.

The other principal transport base in Germany under the command of United States Air Forces, Europe (USAFE), was Weisbaden, which had also been one of the Luftwaffe's top fighter airfields during the war. In 1948 it was the home of the 60th Troop Carrier Group, which on paper comprised the 10th, 12th and 333rd Troop Carrier Squadrons. In fact, the 10th TCS was unmanned. It was the 60th TCG which, in April, had carried out an experimental mini-Airlift to Berlin on General LeMay's instructions.

The American Airlift operation really began with a telephone call from General Clay to General LeMay on the morning of 24 June. Would it be feasible, Clay wanted to know, for USAFE to airlift 500 or 700 tons a day from Rhein-Main or Wiesbaden to Tempelhof over a period of maybe four weeks? LeMay replied that it would and at once set the machinery in motion, appointing Brigadier-General Joseph Smith to command the operation. At this point, the task was to supply the US garrison in Berlin, not the city's population, and LeMay indicated that it would last 45 days. The USAF public

Left and below left *The Douglas C-47 was the mainstay of the USAF's Operation 'Vittles' during the early weeks of the Airlift, but was withdrawn at the end of September 1948 when the C-54 took over.*

Bottom left *Douglas C-47 taking off from Wiesbaden in the early days of the Airlift.*

Right *General Lucius D. Clay, the US Military Governor in Germany, took immediate steps to strengthen the US armed forces in case the Berlin crisis developed into a hot war.*

relations people, with their penchant for the dramatic, wanted to call the Airlift Operation 'Lifeline', but a more moderate view won the day and it became Operation 'Vittles'.

Between them, the 60th and 61st Troop Carrier Groups had eighty C-47s. Within hours, the word went out to various other USAFE locations and 22 more C-47s were added to the Airlift fleet, making a total of 102 — with the result that more than one US military VIP found himself without his personal transport aircraft.

On the first day of Operation 'Vittles', thirty-two C-47 sorties carried eighty tons of supplies to Berlin, mostly fresh milk, flour and medicines. Three weeks later the US total had risen to over 1,500 tons a day — a considerable achievement, for Rhein-Main and Wiesbaden lay 267 and 281 miles (430 and 452 km) from Berlin respectively. Nevertheless, this early phase of Operation 'Vittles' was not very well organized, for the aircrews involved had no experience in running a shuttle service of this type and administrative personnel of the Operations Division, HQ USAFE, had little idea about how the Airlift was to be organized in order to derive the maximum use from the aircraft and to provide the necessary rest periods for their crews. After a month, exhaustion was beginning to set in and pilots were being re-assigned to flying duties from ground tours to give the established aircrew some time off.

It was a highly unsatisfactory situation, and one which required expertise in the organization of large-scale shuttle air transport operations. It arrived on 26 July in the shape of General William H. Tunner, who had been appointed to command Operation 'Vittles' by the USAF Chief of Staff and who, as mentioned earlier, had commanded the air supply operation over 'The Hump' to China during the war. Tunner was not impressed by what he saw in Germany.

'My first overall impression was that the situation was just as I had anticipated — a real cowboy operation. Few people knew what they would be doing the next day. Neither flight crews nor ground crews knew how long they'd be there, or the schedules that they were working. Everything was temporary. I went out to Wiesbaden Air Base, looked around, then hopped a plane to Berlin. Confusion everywhere.'

One of Tunner's priorities was to get the administration right. Control of Operation 'Vittles' on his arrival was vested in what was known as the HQ Berlin Airlift Task Force, USAFE, at Wiesbaden, and on 29 July this was re-designated Airlift Task Force (Provisional) and made a separate entity, although it was still dependent on USAFE for many administrative functions. Tunner also realized that some form of unified control was necessary to co-ordinate the RAF and USAF efforts, which at that time were proceeding independently. When the subject was first discussed there was some difference of opinion over how far the integration of command should go. While one school believed that co-ordination of air traffic control was all that was necessary, another held that one office should be charged with the overall operational control. The question was not finally resolved until 15 October 1948, when the Combined Airlift Task Force was established.

Responsibility for providing the supplies that were to be flown into Berlin, establishing the necessary railheads, receiving supplies at the terminal points, and all handling and transportation on the ground was assigned to the US Army, and an Army Liaison Officer was appointed to Airlift Task Force HQ at Wiesbaden. Later, an Army Airlift Support Command was organized under one Army commander.

The 60th and 61st Troop Carrier Groups were initially charged with flying the maximum number of missions to Berlin. However, the requirement for 4,500 tons per day to supply the western sectors of Berlin soon made it apparent that the three-ton capacity of the C-47 was not adequate. By 1 July, the addition of two Douglas C-54s to the fleet marked the beginning of a heavy support force which, by 1 January 1949, was to grow to 201 USAF and 24 Navy aircraft.

The C-54, which had been adapted during the war from the DC-4 civil airliner to meet the requirements of the US armed forces, had first flown in 1942 and begun to enter service in quantity by the end of that year. Later, it had been selected as the primary USAAF type for the carriage of freight and passengers from the United States to destinations in Europe and the Pacific. Powered by four Pratt & Whitney Twin Wasp radial engines, the C-54 Skymaster cruised at 180 knots and carried a payload of just under ten tons. The US Navy version of the Skymaster, which was also to play its part in the Airlift, was designated R5D. (In fact, the Military Air Transport Service (MATS), which had been formed from the wartime Air Transport Command on 1 June 1948 under the command of Major-General Laurence Kuter, had absorbed the Naval Air Transport Service's facilities. In June 1948 these comprised three squadrons of R4Ds (C-47s) and three of R5Ds.)

The ink was barely dry on Kuter's first batch of orders when he was asked to

A C-54 approaching Tempelhof over the shattered Berlin suburbs.

switch a substantial part of his C-54 force to Europe to augment the Airlift, a preliminary move made by Tunner before leaving to take up his appointment at Wiesbaden. As a result, on the day of Tunner's arrival — 26 July — the 48th Troop Carrier Squadron received orders to deploy its nine C-54s, together with 48 officers and 88 enlisted men, from its usual base at Bergstrom, Texas, to Rhein-Main. The nine aircraft were en route for Germany that same day. Similar orders were issued to the 54th Troop Carrier Squadron at Anchorage, Alaska; the 19th Troop Carrier Squadron at Hickam Field, Honolulu; and the 20th Troop Carrier Squadron from Panama. By the middle of August 54 C-54s had been assembled at Rhein-Main, bringing the total number of US aircraft committed to the Airlift at that time to 161 — various accidents having taken their toll of some of the C-47s in the meantime.

In parallel with this increase in the Airlift Task Force, plans were going ahead to increase the numbers of American combat aircraft available in Europe. Once the Airlift had been established on a large scale, the Russians had to be dissuaded from interfering with it. This could only be achieved by dispatching modern combat aircraft to Europe with the utmost priority, and that meant the Boeing B-29, which had the capability to hit the Russians hard. In fact, only a handful of Strategic Air Command's B-29s were equipped for the carriage and release of atomic weapons at this time, and the entire US stockpile of atomic bombs in 1948 comprised two weapons, built in case they were required for further attacks on Japan in 1945 and subsequently placed in storage.

The Russians, however, were presumed to be unaware of this, and the presence of even a small force of B-29s in Britain would, it was thought, have a considerable deterrent effect. Atomic weapons aside, the B-29 carried a formidable conventional bomb load and had sufficient range to hit targets deep

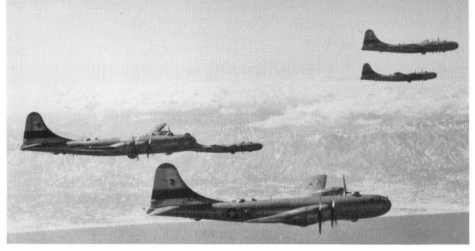

The Berlin crisis led to the deployment of the first Boeing B-29 Superfortresses to Britain as a strategic deterrent, and marked the beginning of a powerful USAF presence which is still crucial to Europe's defence.

inside western Russia — a fact of which the Russians were aware through their own experience with their captured examples.

Agreement had existed since 1946, though not on a formal basis, between the British Air Ministry and the USAF for the use of British air bases by conventionally armed American bombers in the event of a war threat in Europe. Its implementation now was little more than a formality to which the Attlee Government readily agreed, and on 16 July 1948 a joint announcement was made by the Air Ministry and the USAF to the effect that two B-29 medium bomber groups, totalling sixty aircraft, were flying from the USA to bases in England 'for a period of temporary duty'; that this movement was 'part of the normal long-range flight training programme instituted over a year ago by the US Strategic Air Command' to which these groups belonged; and that the squadrons would be based at Marham in Norfolk and Waddington in Lincolnshire under the operational control of General Curtis LeMay, Commanding General of USAFE. It was also announced that C-54 aircraft would be transporting maintenance men and supplies to the UK, that each B-29 would carry regular and spare crews, and that about 1,500 men would be involved in the training.

To support the B-29 groups on their period of 'temporary duty' in England the Americans needed a supply and maintenance depot. The site selected was Burtonwood, in Cheshire, which in 1942 had been the central repair depot for all American-built aircraft and engines used by the RAF and by the USAAF units which had then just arrived to join the air offensive against Germany. It was rather ironic that Burtonwood would now, through its work of maintaining transport aircraft in 1948-49, become a crucial factor in keeping up the flow of supplies to the former Reich capital.

The repair and maintenance facilities had been greatly expanded during the war years, and when the war ended a skeleton USAAF staff had remained to look after existing stocks of American equipment. In January 1946 the RAF's No 276 Maintenance Unit had moved in, creating additional facilities. The site's wartime workshops and installations were still intact, so it was a logical step to re-activate them to help meet the current crisis. Consequently, in the summer of 1948, USAF technical personnel were moved into the base to prepare support facilities for Project 'Skincoat', as the SAC deployments were to be called.

On 17 July 1948, thirty B-29s of the 28th Bomb Group, the first to be deployed, flew into their British base — not, as it turned out, either Marham or Waddington, but Scampton in Lincolnshire, which had recently been vacated by the Lancasters and Wellingtons of the Bomber Command Instrument Rating and Examining Flight. The next day, thirty more B-29s of the 2nd Bomb Group arrived at Lakenheath in Suffolk, and on 8 August the 307th Bomb Group, comprising the 370th and 371st Bombardment Squadrons, brought its Superfortresses to Marham.

Meanwhile, the rapid reinforcement of General Curtis LeMay's depleted combat elements in Europe had got under way. In the third week of July, sixteen Lockheed F-80 Shooting Stars of the 56th Fighter Group, commanded by Lieutenant-Colonel David Schilling, left their home base at Selfridge, Michigan, on the first leg of a journey that took them via Bangor, Maine, to Goose Bay in Labrador. From there they flew to Bluie West, in Greenland, in 1 hour 50 minutes, then to Reykjavik, Iceland, in 1 hour 45 minutes, and from Iceland to Stornoway in 1 hour 40 minutes, making a total transatlantic flight time of 5 hours 15 minutes. From Stornoway the F-80s flew to Odiham, in Hampshire, where they refuelled for the last leg of their flight to their base in Germany.

This was not the first transatlantic flight by jet aircraft; that had been

The Berlin crisis also saw the rapid deployment of F-80 Shooting Star jet fighter-bombers to USAFE bases. These aircraft could carry a formidable weapons load, as this photograph shows.

completed eight days earlier, on 12 July, by six de Havilland Vampire F 3s of No 54 Squadron, RAF, which had left Odiham to carry out a goodwill tour of Canada and the United States. They had followed the same route as the F-80s, though in the opposite direction, and it had taken them three hours longer, partly because of their lower cruising speed and partly because they encountered jet streams of up to 200 mph (322 km/h) at their cruising altitude of 35,000 ft (10,668 m).

On 14 August 75 more Shooting Stars arrived in Britain, this time by sea aboard the aircraft carrier USS *Sicily*. The fighters were offloaded in the Clyde and taken to Prestwick for overhaul before flying on to their destinations on the Continent.

On 25 August the US Air Force announced that the contingent at Burtonwood was to be expanded to 2,500 personnel under the command of Lieutenant-Colonel Walter Ott. This would turn Burtonwood into the principal USAF base in Britain, and it would be responsible not only for supporting the three B-29 Groups — the latter under the command of Major General Leon Johnson — but also for providing facilities for the supply and maintenance of American aircraft engaged in the rapidly expanding Operation 'Vittles', the Berlin Airlift. A few days later, it was revealed that the number of US military aircraft in Europe — including the B-29s and the transports involved in the Airlift — had risen to 466, and that the number of USAF personnel had increased to 18,000. About 6,000 of these, it was stated, would be based in Britain before the end of the year.

At this time the principal maintenance depot for the USAF aircraft engaged in the Berlin Airlift was Oberpfaffenhofen, in the American Zone, where the necessary 200-hour inspections were carried out. But facilities at this depot were primitive; aircraft were washed down with a mixture of kerosene and water on open-air ramps because there was no adequate hangarage, and with winter approaching it was clear that this procedure would soon become unacceptable. Top priority was therefore given to the rapid expansion of the Burtonwood facilities with the help of experienced technicians from the big US Air Materiel Command centre at Tinker Air Force Base, near Oklahoma City, who arrived in the somewhat cooler climes of Cheshire early in September and set about reactivating the wartime maintenance facilities. Gradually, they set up a three-quarter-mile-long assembly line on which eight aircraft a day could be cleaned by commerical-type vacuum cleaners and then hosed down with detergent.

The smooth operation of the USAF facility at Burtonwood during the months that followed was crucial to the Airlift operation as a whole; it is no exaggeration to say that the Airlift could not have succeeded without it. After the withdrawal of all USAF C-47s from the Airlift at the end of September 1948, Burtonwood handled only the big four-engined C-54 Skymasters, which required some twenty man-hours of maintenance for every flying hour. Every C-54 engaged in the Airlift underwent checks after every 50, 100 and 150 hours' flying, the 100-hour check involving a change of spark plugs and oil.

These checks were carried out at the aircraft's home base, but for the 200-hour inspection it was flown to Burtonwood for a six-phase check. This comprised washing and cleaning the aircraft; running up the engines; carrying out maintenance work on engines, pipes and ignition; servicing the electrical system, instruments, cables and rigging; and inspecting the hydraulics, wheels, brakes and tyres. Finally, each C-54 was subjected to a rigorous pre-flight check and cleared for its return operations. (The RAF, it should be noted, had its own Transport Command Major Servicing Unit at RAF Honington, Suffolk.)

Meanwhile, the B-29 groups in Britain had been carrying out a systematic training programme designed to familiarize the crews with their European environment — although many had seen service here during the war years — and in carrying out simulated bombing attacks on targets around the United Kingdom and in western Europe. The original three groups remained in England for ninety days of temporary duty (TDY), setting the pattern for other Strategic Air Command Units that were to follow. At Scampton, the 28th Bomb Group's B-29s were replaced by those of the 301st Bomb Group. These departed in turn on 15 January 1949, whereupon Scampton reverted to RAF use with the arrival of No 230 Operational Conversion Unit's Lancasters and Lincolns.

The other two airfields allocated to Strategic Air Command, Marham and Lakenheath, continued with TDY detachments; at Marham, for example, the 307th Bomb Group was replaced in November 1948 by the 97th Bomb Group, comprising the 340th and 371st Bombardment Squadrons. Only one other SAC B-29 unit, the 22nd Bomb Group (2nd, 19th and 408th Bombardment Squadrons) was destined to use Marham; subsequent TDY detachments all operated the more advanced Boeing B-50.

Back in Germany, the establishment of a large C-54 force at Rhein-Main soon caused problems of overcrowding, and in August the decision was taken to move part of the C-54 fleet to Fassberg, in the British Zone. The move involved the 60th Troop Carrier Wing (Heavy) in its entirety, the units involved being the 313th Troop Carrier Group with its 11th, 29th, 47th and 48th Troop Carrier Squadrons, the 513th Air Base Group and the 513th Maintenance and Support Group. In terms of personnel, the numbers totalled 540 officers, 1,400 senior NCOs and about 4,000 GIs.

The arrival of the Americans at Fassberg from 20 August 1948, when the first three squadrons flew in, caused a few headaches for the station commander, Group Captain Biggar. To prepare for their arrival, he organized the construction of a new PSP loading area, a mile and a quarter long and 100 yd wide (2,012 by 91.4m), capable of accommodating 65 Skymasters; the work was completed in just nineteen days. The USAF commander of flying operations at Fassberg was Lieutenant-Colonel Paul A. Jones, with whom Biggar got on well. The whole USAF contingent, however, was under the command of a full Colonel, and the fact that he was of equal rank to Biggar was bound to cause problems. The official Air Ministry report, compiled at the close of the Airlift, summed up the command situation at Fassberg very well:

'The USAF wing... was responsible to 1st ALTF for operations and technical matters. This meant that there were two senior officers of the same rank, neither responsible to the other and neither having a very clear idea as to where his responsibilities began or ended. The situation was bound, sooner or later, to cause minor difficulties. To counter this, an experiment was carried out at Fassberg, where the command of the station, including the RAF administrative element, was vested in the USAF Wing Commander. This experiment worked very well, but it must be recorded that this was largely due to the personality and efforts of the US Commander (*ie Paul Jones*). A great handicap in the operation of an integrated RAF/USAF force is the lack of any legal machinery for the maintenance of discipline. It would be an excellent thing if some form of agreement, such as exists between the British Dominions and the UK, could be entered into between the US and ourselves. It is of interest to note that, under existing conditions, the only action that can be taken in the event of insubordination or assault between members of the two Services is the preferment of a civil charge.'

Inter-Service niggles, plus the fact that conditions at Fassberg were more primitive than those generally taken for granted by the Americans, made the RAF station generally unpopular with them. Neither were the Americans popular with the British personnel, who amounted to about thirty RAF and Army officers and 450 other ranks and who were consequently heavily outnumbered. Fortunately, the officers in charge of the operation were ruthlessly determined that all that mattered was the carriage of coal to Berlin — coal that was humped to the Skymasters by 5,000 German civilians who were housed in a labour camp two miles (3.2 km) from the airfield, under the command of an Army officer.

On 16 September 1948, five Fairchild C-82 transport aircraft were assigned to the Airlift for the purpose of carrying heavy and unwieldy cargo. Later, these aircraft were to prove invaluable in flying heavy construction equipment to Berlin for use in the building of the new airfield at Tegel. The C-82, with its hangar-like cargo compartment and clamshell rear loading doors was an ideal tool for the Airlift, but was not available in sufficient numbers to make a greater contribution. A month earlier, single Douglas C-74 Globemaster had also joined the Airlift; it began operations from Rhein-Main on 17 August, carrying twenty tons of flour to Gatow. The C-74 had reverse pitch, and because the taxi track at Gatow was not wide or strong enough to support it a technique was developed whereby the massive aircraft taxied backwards down the runway and reversed into its parking position. Unfortunately, only a single squadron was then in service, and one aircraft was all that could be spared — although Globemasters provided invaluable service in ferrying supplies and spares across the Atlantic to Burtonwood. (The C-74, which was later developed into the C-124A Globemaster II, heralded a new generation of heavy-lift transport aircraft capable of carrying 200 fully-equipped troops or large quantities of freight over vast distances.)

A typical USAF Airlift pilot made two or three flights to Berlin during each

The USAF used a solitary C-97 Stratofreighter for a short time on Operation 'Vittles', the aircraft eventually being withdrawn after being damaged in a landing accident.

period of duty, which required between six and eight hours of flying time. He also spent another six to eight hours on standby. A pilot often had to wait three or four hours after reporting for duty before he was scheduled for his first take-off. He then had to await his take-off turn, wait for the unloading and sometimes reloading of his aircraft in Berlin, then on return to his home base wait for the second load to be put aboard, and perhaps also wait while his aircraft underwent some on-the-line maintenance. After this ten to sixteen-hour tour of duty, pilots had between twelve and twenty hours' free time. Most pilots worked on a seven-day week schedule, with very little leave, and it was not uncommon for a pilot to fly for four or five months without any leave at all — and this on a seven-day week schedule. Some pilots, at peak periods remained on duty for as long as 36 hours. One pilot who experienced this flew two consecutive missions to Berlin, and on completion of the second mission the weather was so bad at his home base — Wiesbaden — that he had to wait twelve hours at Tempelhof in the hope that the weather would lift. He was then diverted to Fassberg and flew two additional missions, hauling coal to Berlin. Returning from the second Fassberg mission, after about 36 hours without any rest time, he reported that all four crew members aboard the C-54 fell asleep and the aircraft flew itself on autopilot for some time.

Living conditions for personnel assigned to the airlift were very crowded, and this was particularly bad for enlisted men and for the personnel at Rhein-Main. Very few Airlift personnel had their families in Germany, and many of those who did had not been able to obtain family quarters within commuting distance of their base. In general, living conditions during duty hours resembled those of a combat-type operation. The Airlift ran both day and night without any significant change, and therefore offered a unique opportunity for evaluating causative factors such as the probability of day and night accidents. Two-thirds of all accidents occurred at night, and some resulted in the build-up of a relatively simple chain of circumstances. For example, one of the major contributing factors leading to a serious accident involving a C-54 was the lack of standardization in the mode of operation of the controls in the different models of that aircraft. The report of this accident reads as follows:

'A C-54E aircraft took off from Celle at 2017Z on a routine airlift mission. The pilot followed the normal routine procedure of flying straight ahead for two minutes and then turning onto a heading of 350° for one minute. Shortly after this the number four engine began to cut out, and immediately thereafter the number two engine did likewise. At 2020Z the pilot advised the tower of his difficulty and requested permission to return to Celle. A moment later the numbers two and four engines cut out completely and both propellers were feathered. The pilot did not establish GCA contact, and GCA was unable to pick him up on their scopes. A third engine then cut out. At that time the aircraft was too low for the occupants to bale out. At about 2030Z it crashed and burned. All three crew members escaped.

'At the scene of the crash, the fuel selectors were found to be in the forward or auxiliary ON position. In the C-54 Model E and G aircraft, the main ON position is half-way forward on the quadrant. On the C-54D, however, the main tanks are ON when the selectors are in the fully forward position. This accident was due specifically to confusion in the operation of controls, the C-54E having been flown by personnel who had been flying the C-54D.'

A typical mission involving a USAF C-54 would unfold as follows. Each group established its own duty schedule for flying personnel; this varied from group to group, some flying twelve hours on and twelve off, some twelve on and 24 off, and others eight on and sixteen off, depending on the prevailing conditions. However, because of maintenance problems, it was not possible to stick to a rigid duty schedule. Usually, each pilot was informed the day before of the time he was required to report to the flight line. He might then fly immediately, or else be faced with a wait of several hours, depending on the number of aircraft in use. Upon arriving at the ready room, pilots were briefed on expected weather and winds, and given a flight plan detailing relevant en route information such as headings, times over points en route and so on. They were also informed of any unusual conditions or activity going on in the corridor. When the C-54 assigned to a particular crew was brought on line, a taxi and take-off time was assigned to it by Operations. This time had to be adhered to very closely, so that aircraft from different bases could slot into their assigned places in the flow of traffic along the corridor.

Crews reported to their aircraft twenty to thirty minutes prior to taxi time. A preflight check was completed, and the load checked with the loading crew. The engine run-up was carried out after the aircraft had taxied to the end of the runway; after informing the tower that he was ready for take-off, the pilot then awaited instructions, including the en route altitude through the corridor. Cleared for take-off, he rolled the C-54 on to the runway, applied power and immediately turned over the power settings to the copilot or engineer. Climb was made at 155 mph, 400-450 ft/min (249 km/h, 122-137 m/min).

On a typical flight from Rhein-Main, aircraft climbed straight ahead to 900 ft (274 m) on the QNH before turning south and homing on to the Darmstadt Beacon, crossing Darmstadt at 3,000 ft (914 m). This required approximately five minutes. From Darmstadt the pilot homed on to the Aschaffenburg Beacon, eight to ten minutes away, climbing to the assigned altitude of 5,000 or 6,000 ft (1,524 or 1,829 m). On reaching his assigned altitude, IAS was increased to 170 mph (273 km/h), which was maintained throughout the corridor.

On reaching the Aschaffenburg Beacon the pilot then turned towards the Fulda Range station; this leg required about fifteen minutes. Navigation aids at Fulda included a low frequency range and a VAR range. When crossing the Fulda Range the pilot transmitted, in clear language, his time, altitude and in-flight conditions (IFR or VFR) for the benefit of aircraft ahead of and behind him. He then tracked outbound on the Fulda Range using either the low frequency range or the VAR range for a minimum of ten minutes, at which point he should have been able to establish a definite heading to take him through the corridor. From that point until he picked up the Tempelhof Range — either low frequency or VAR — the pilot had to fly established headings or navigate, if possible, by pilotage, relying on the Gun Post fixer station (radar post) for any additional flight information.

Forty minutes after passing Fulda, or at the Kornorn intersection — an ILS range leg closing the corridor at an angle of 90 degrees — the pilot called Tempelhof Airways, giving a position report and obtaining further information. It was at this point that Tempelhof's CPS-5 radar was able to pick up the incoming aircraft. The pilot was usually instructed to turn right or left for one minute to assist the radar operator in identifying the aircraft. If the pilot was off course, this was the moment he was brought back into his correct place in the corridor. Instructions were transmitted governing letdown procedures. On reaching the Tempelhof Range the pilot passed a position report to Tempelhof Airways, whereupon he was instructed to contact either Tempelhof Tower or Tempelhof GCA, depending on the weather.

GCA was always considered to be the primary standard approach, regardless of weather, and was normally used whether it was needed or not. For a westerly landing, the aircraft was vectored on to a heading of 360 degrees at an altitude of 2,000 ft (609 m) for one minute, then turned on to a downwind leg of 90 degrees, descending to 1,500 ft (457 m) for one minute. This was followed by a vector on to a base leg of 180 degrees until the aircraft was abeam the end of the runway, when it was turned on to final approach and instructions given for the pilot to contact GCA final or the tower. The procedure was essentially the same for easterly landings, except that a left-hand instead of a right-hand pattern was flown and the downwind leg was about three minutes instead of one. This brought the aircraft to a position some six miles (9.5 km) north-west of Tempelhof before it was turned on to its base leg heading of 180 degrees.

Minimum altitude at Tempelhof was 400 ft (122 m), but it was left up to the pilot to determine whether he was VFR at that altitude. All aircraft despatched

A C-54 approaching to land at Tempelhof through the murk of a Berlin winter. The pylons, made from pierced steel planking, mount high-intensity approach lights.

for Tempelhof, Tegel or Gatow were instructed to make their approach regardless of weather conditions, but pilots were instructed not to go below the minimum altitudes for the different fields unless they were VFR on reaching those altitudes.

Due to the rapidity with which weather changes could occur in the Berlin area, the weather would often lift for just long enough to allow up to half a dozen aircraft to slip in before the minimum ceiling returned. Aircraft continued to be despatched from outlying bases to Berlin regardless of weather conditions at their destination until it became very certain that no further landings would be possible for three or four hours.

Upon landing, the aircraft was met immediately by a 'follow me' Jeep which led them to a space on the loading ramp. Here they were met by the unloading crew, a weather officer and — the most welcome sight of all for the crew — a portable snack bar. Unloading was accomplished by a German crew of twelve to fifteen men and usually required twenty to thirty minutes. If no return load was to be taken from Berlin, the aircraft was started up and taxied to its take-off position as soon as the unloading operation was completed.

Aircraft were despatched by the tower at three or five minute intervals depending on the weather, and instructed to climb to alternate altitudes of 7,500 and 8,500 ft (2,286 and 2,591 m). Two runways were used at Tempelhof, one for landing and the other for take-off. Enough time was allowed between aircraft landing and those taking off to permit adequate separation between aircraft in the event of a missed approach. Aircraft missing their approach at Tempelhof might be diverted to Tegel or Gatow, depending on whether or not there was sufficient break in the traffic pattern at those airfields, or alternatively directed to return to their point of origin.

After taking off from Tempelhof the aircraft turned at 700 ft (213 m) on to a heading of either 255 or 260 degrees, depending on whether the take-off was easterly or westerly, and homed on to the Wannsee Beacon. If the take-off was westerly the aircraft climbed immediately to 3,500 ft (1,067 m); in the easterly case it had to remain below 1,000 ft (305 m) until it was at a point identified by the 'A' Quadrant of the Tempelhof Range, ensuring that it was safely clear of the traffic patterns of landing aircraft. Passing the Wannsee Beacon at 3,500 ft (1,067 m) the pilot then homed on to the Braunschweig Beacon, climbing to his assigned altitude and establishing 180 mph (290 km/h) IAS.

Over Braunschweig a postion report was again transmitted in clear language, as at Fulda on the inbound flight, for the information of other aircraft in the corridors. At Braunschweig the pilot turned left and homed on to the Fritzlar Beacon, 95 miles (153 km) away, and on reaching this he gave a position report to Fritzlar Airways. On leaving Fritzlar, aircraft reported to Frankfurt Airways, which gave instructions on letdown procedures and whether to contact Rhein-Main tower or GCA, and continued on to Staden Beacon. At the Staden Beacon, contact was made with either GCA or the tower, airspeed was decreased to 140 mph (225 km/h) and a descent to 2,500 ft (762 m) was begun, the aircraft crossing Offenbach Beacon at that altitude. Here aircraft were vectored by GCA on to their final approach heading if landing to the west; if landing to the east, they were vectored to a point seven miles (11 km) west of the airfield and then turned on to final approach at 2,000 ft (609 m).

Here, as at Tempelhof, the primary landing approach was GCA, and GCA approaches were normally made regardless of weather. Minima at Rhein-Main were 300 ft and half a mile (91 and 805 m). On initial contact with GCA the pilot reported the condition of his aircraft and whether or not he was loaded. Aircraft which required no maintenance before making another trip were reported as 'positive', those that required maintenance as 'negative'. Similarly, loaded aircraft were reported as 'positive' and unloaded aircraft as 'negative' — so a loaded aircraft requiring no maintenance would be reported as 'positive, positive'.

If the aircraft was serviceable on landing it was immediately assigned another taxi and take-off time. The pilot reported to Operations, where he was given another flight plan — then, thirty minutes before the scheduled taxi time, it was back to the C-54 to rejoin his crew for yet another haul into the beleaguered city.

All navigation on 'Vittles' flights was done by the pilots, using radio aids and information received from ground radar stations. Unlike the RAF, USAF transport aircraft engaged in the Airlift did not carry navigators, which on occasion caused problems. Although aircraft were despatched to Berlin at precise three, four or five-minute intervals, they often failed to maintain this separation in the corridors. As weather conditions deteriorated with the approach of winter, USAF observers spent many hours in the Tempelhof radar room, watching aircraft come into range of the search radar. Frequently, two aircraft appeared on the CRT almost simultaneously, in the same corridor.

Scarcely an hour went by without three aircraft approaching Berlin virtually abreast of one another. At a later period of the Airlift, when fatigue was taking a severe toll of pilot efficiency, it was noted that some pilots from Wiesbaden were making no apparent effort to maintain a temporal separation from Rhein-Main aircraft, but were flying at different altitudes.

There were various reasons contributing to the inability of pilots to maintain precise separation, including variations in the calibration of airspeed indicators, variations in compass calibration, variations in the ability of different pilots to hold accurate airspeed and heading, and variations in the procedure used to determine and report times over the radio beacons en route. Sorting out this haphazard spacing, which many US staff officers believed was the most critical factor limiting the frequency with which aircraft could be despatched to Berlin, was the task of the CPS-5 search radar at Tempelhof — although it should be mentioned that pilots held an opposite view, most being strongly convinced that inadequate landing facilities were the root cause of most bottlenecks.

The CPS-5 radar antenna was located on top of the Tempelhof airfield buildings, the control room being directly below the control tower. In it were six twelve-inch (30.5 cm) remote viewing scopes and large display boards on which was shown all traffic inbound for the three Berlin landing fields. During the first few months of its operation, the CPS-5 was operated by pilots, but in March 1949 the operation was gradually turned over to enlisted personnel whose qualifications were similar to those of GCA operators.

Below left *American, British and French air traffic controllers at their places in the Operations Room of the Berlin Air Safety Centre in the Allied Control Commission building. The Soviet controller, Senior Lieutenant Komarov, refused to be photographed with the rest.*

Below right *Senior Lieutenant Komarov sits in isolation, answering the telephone on the left of this picture.*

There were no mid-air collisions during the Airlift period while the CPS-5 was in operation. The radar undoubtedly contributed greatly to air safety in the crowded Berlin area. When as many as three aircraft appeared simultaneously at the seventy-mile (113 km) outer range ring of the radar scope, operators could and did sort them out into minimum two-minute spacing intervals before they reached the Tempelhof radio range. The successful spacing of incoming aircraft at intervals sufficient to permit GCA to land them was an outstanding achievement of the approach control radar and those who operated it. The biggest accolade came from the pilots themselves, who attributed to the CPS-5 a large share of the credit for the successful operation of the Airlift throughout the winter of 1948-49. After receiving their initial instructions, pilots almost invariably asked the controller to supply their forward separation; the fact that Tempelhof could tell them precisely the number of miles between them and the aircraft ahead was undoubtedly an important psychological factor, enabling pilots to concentrate on their flying and navigation without having to worry about collisions.

Nevertheless, radar approach control was a recent art, and it was hardly surprising that a number of rough spots showed up. When an approaching aircraft first reported by radio to Tempelhof, for example, the only method available for positive identification was to ask it to make a turn and to observe which blip on the radar scope changed course as prescribed. This usually required from thirty seconds to one minute to implement, and if several aircraft appeared on the scope at about the same time and in the same area it was important to identify them quickly and positively.

There was no standby radar equipment at Tempelhof. Failure of the generators or any other critical element of the system caused the CPS-5 to go off the air, with potentially serious consequences to the Berlin traffic if it happened without warning. The GCA radar provided a limited overlap with the CPS-5, but was inadequate to do the job normally handled by the latter. However, the philosophy followed throughout the Airlift was to anticipate emergencies and to establish pre-set plans for handling them. Pilots were fully briefed on how to proceed in the event of radio failure, missed approaches and so on.

A number of emergency landings had been handled by GCA teams in Berlin without mishap, but one situation that was dreaded by all personnel was the complete failure of all radar facilities in the Berlin area. Some of the most critical periods during the Airlift occurred during the changeover from one routine procedure to another, such as times when GCA had just gone off the air or returned to the air, times when crew shift changes were taking place, or when the landing direction was being changed.

The GCA equipment used on the Airlift was rather old. Most sets were of the AN/MPN-1 variety; one CPN-4 set was in use at Tempelhof, but was not in operation as much as the MPN-1. Despite the ageing equipment, however, GCA did a sterling job of work, and it is useful to recall that the weather minima that were in force during the winter of 1948-49 were: Tempelhof — 400 ft (122 m) ceiling and one mile (1.6 km) visibility; Wiesbaden and Rhein-Main — 300 ft (91 m) ceiling and half a mile (805 m) visibility; all other fields — 200 ft (61 m) ceiling and half a mile visibility. Tempelhof landings were more difficult than at other fields due to the presence of five-storey apartment buildings around the field. The glide path at Tempelhof was four degrees, and this required a rate of descent of 750 ft/minute (299 m/minute). The four-degree glide path brought incoming aircraft to within less than 100 ft (30 m) of the roofs of the buildings surrounding the field. The buildings also made it necessary to locate the GCA at the end of the runway that was farthest from the approaching aircraft so that the radar could 'see' over them. The buildings were definite psychological hazards; all pilots tended to come in high at Tempelhof, and GCA final approach controllers spent an inordinate amount of time in cajoling pilots to 'come on down'. Three aircraft (C-54s) were wrecked at Tempelhof due to landing too far down the runway, but none was wrecked through landing short.

The record achieved in landing aircraft in Berlin during the winter of 1948-49 was an outstanding one. GCA played a key role in this achievement, with aircraft landing at four or five-minute intervals throughout the winter. At Tempelhof, for example, a total of 13,947 IFR approaches were made from September 1948 to the end of March 1949. Of these, seventeen per cent were made with weather below IFR minima, and only slightly over two per cent of approaches were missed. However, although the GCA facilities were generally approved by the pilots, rather more criticism was levelled at them than at the CPS-5. This was probably due to the fact that pilots were more concerned about the actual landing than the approach to it. Often, GCA crews landed aircraft at two-minute intervals as a matter of routine, which was necessary when aircraft approached Berlin at considerably shorter intervals than their despatch intervals. The GCA controllers appeared to experience little difficulty with two-minute intervals; at Tempelhof, pilots intercepted the glide path at an altitude of 1,200 ft (366 m), or roughly one and a half minutes from touchdown. As long as the final GCA approach controller could establish communication with the pilot in time to give him a heading and brief preliminary instructions before the aircraft intercepted the glide path, usually no difficulty was experienced in completing the landing.

The GCA approach controller also handled aircraft at two-minute intervals, which often meant that he was directing three aircraft in the traffic pattern at the same time: one aircraft approximately over the Tempelhof range station, one turning on the downwind leg, and one turning on to final approach. At Tempelhof, the traffic pattern utilized one-minute legs. Each stage of the Berlin landing operation was critically dependent on the preceding stage for traffic separation, so if the approach controller turned aircraft accurately on to final approach, there was little subsequent difficulty in maintaining the correct separation around the traffic pattern.

The capacity of the CPS-5 radar was likewise limited by the spacing which pilots themselves were able to maintain in the corridors. The CPS-5 could space aircraft at two-minute intervals provided they came into radar range not more than three abreast. Since aircraft were despatched at four-minute intervals, and since they could actually have been handled safely and efficiently at two-minute intervals, there was a considerable built-in safety factor, and most emergencies could be effectively handled by proper use of this reserve time.

One of the serious limitations of GCA was the critical role played by voice communication. GCA controllers could convey only a limited amount of information by voice. The limited number of voice communication channels available, and the time needed to shift from one channel to another, was a further problem. Yet another serious problem was the correct identification of aircraft, which applied both to GCA and to the CPS-5. The following critical incident, related by a 'Vittles' C-54 pilot, illustrates the serious consequences of such identification failures.

'I was making a GCA run on Rhein-Main with the weather down to, or below, GCA minima. I was given directions by the initial GCA controller and turned over to the GCA final controller. He continued to give me directions until I was down to about 75 ft (23 m) above ground level. At that time I was directed to take over visually and land. Fortunately, at that moment I broke out to find myself over the middle of Frankfurt, about ten miles (16 km) north of the field. A similar incident happened to me at a later date. I believe that these errors occurred because the ground controller was giving instructions to the aircraft in front of me, but using my callsign.'

Several reports of similar incidents were received from other pilots, one of whom said: 'In several cases during poor radio reception, the GCA operator gave preliminary instructions for intercepting the glide path and beginning the final letdown. These preliminary instructions were mistaken for instructions to begin the actual letdown. As a result, the glidepath was intercepted at too low an altitude. After experiencing this a number of times, we developed the habit of holding constant altitude, waiting for verification and instructions to start the letdown on the glidepath. Unfortunately, this procedure sometimes resulted in going too high.'

The presence of clutter on the radar scope was another problem that dogged GCA operation. Clutter was particularly bad at Tempelhof because of its location in the centre of Berlin. On many occasions, aircraft were momentarily lost to view, usually during the last stage of final approach and particularly when aircraft were passing over the buildings at the perimeter of the field.

There were acute shortages of many specific supply items needed for the Airlift operation. As an example, it was often found necessary, during the winter of 1948-49, to remove small items such as instruments, UV lights, starters and generators from an aircraft that was out for maintenance and install them in another aircraft.

By the beginning of October 1948, the US Military Air Transport Service had no further reserves of C-54s to commit to the Berlin Airlift, and the Airlift Task Force was still short of the 180 aircraft of this type needed to meet the requirement. Two US Navy R5D squadrons, VR-6 and VR-8, were consequently assigned to Operation 'Vittles' from their Pacific bases of Guam and Honolulu at a few hours' notice. The first stage of their flight to Europe was via Moffett Field, in California, where all passenger and VIP R5Ds belonging to the two units were exchanged for R5D freighters drawn from other squadrons. They then flew on to Jacksonville, Florida, to be fitted with extra radio and radar equipment, and finally reached Rhein-Main on 9 November — or at least the first aircraft did, because each machine left Jacksonville individually as soon as its equipment fit was complete.

Each Navy squadron had nine aircraft. At Rhein-Main, VR-6 was assigned to the operational control of the 513th Troop Carrier Group and VR-8 to the 61st Troop Carrier Group. The Navy fliers brought an astonishing degree of expertise and efficiency to the Airlift, and their USAF counterparts were impressed, in particular, by the self-supporting nature of the Navy detachment. Navy technicians were permitted, on the squadron, to carry out all maintenance up to the R5D's 1,000-hour check, whereas the USAF's C-54s had to go to Burtonwood every 200 hours. Much to their disgust, the Navy men were told that their R5Ds would also have to go to Burtonwood for their 200-hour and subsequent checks. The first Navy R5D was duly returned to Burtonwood when its 200-hour check became due. When it came back to Rhein-Main, there was so much wrong with it that its captain refused to accept it as serviceable. After that, whenever an R5D went back to Burtonwood its captain went with it and kept a constant eye on what went on. The standard of servicing improved as a result, and aircraft were returned to Rhein-Main more quickly.

The tonnage lifted to Berlin by the USAF rose steadily. From 26 June to 31 July, 41,188 tons were carried to the city by 8,117 sorties; the August figure was 73,632 tons in 9,769 sorties; in September, 101,871 tons in 12,905 sorties. At the end of that month all C-47s were withdrawn from Operation 'Vittles', which now became exclusively a C-54 operation — with the exception, of

A German worker lifts the millionth sack of coal to arrive in Berlin — compliments of the USAF at Fassberg.

course, of the five C-82s, the lone C-74 and a Boeing C-97A Stratofreighter which was used experimentally for a short time until it suffered a major accident in May 1949.

It was one of many. In July 1948 six C-47s and two C-54s were involved in major accidents, two of which occurred in flight, three on the approach to land and three on the ground. One of the C-47s hit a block of flats while on the approach to Tempelhof on 25 July and crashed in flames in a Berlin street, while another crashed in a field on the approach to Wiesbaden. One C-47 and two C-54s were also involved in minor accidents. In August, major accidents accounted for another three C-47s and two C-54s; one of the C-47s caught fire in mid-air, while two C-54s were wrecked in landing accidents. In September, the figure was five C-47s and one C-54 involved in serious accidents, with three of each type suffering minor accidents. By the end of the year, USAF transport aircraft had been involved in 38 major accidents and 21 minor ones.

A major factor in many of these accidents was the prevailing weather. Many of the MATS crews were unused to the kind of weather conditions prevailing in Europe, and found difficulty in coping with them. Low cloud, fog, freezing rain, turbulence and ice had not been part of their everyday routine until now. It was a problem that had to be met head-on and overcome if the Airlift mission was to succeed.

With this in mind, all Airlift procedures in the early days were planned to enable crews to operate in conditions that were well below the USAF minima. This meant that the Air Weather Service had to be more accurate in its forecasts than ever before; previously, there had been no great operational requirement to know, for example, whether a cloud ceiling was 250 ft (76 m) instead of 200 ft (61 m), or whether visibility was three-quarters instead of half a mile (1,207 instead of 805 m), because in both cases airfields were well below the closed minima. Under the Airlift's urgency this situation was changed. What was needed now was knowledge of the exact ceiling and visibility, for 50 ft or a quarter of a mile (15 or 400 m) could mean the difference between aircraft getting into an airfield or being diverted elsewhere. Moreover, accurate forecasts of ceilings and visibility to these levels were required at least three hours in advance.

To meet the demand, the Air Weather Service concentrated the best of its personnel and equipment in Europe. It was an exercise that was to result in the gathering of much new knowledge and the trial of new techniques which would eventually be of immeasurable value to weather forecasting in the future. Before the Airlift began, Weather Service requirements for MATS and USAFE were met by a single weather squadron. With the Airlift under way, this squadron — the 18th, at Weisbaden — found itself faced with a tremendous increase in workload almost without warning.

The weather stations at Wiesbaden, Rhein-Main and Tempelhof had been able to provide adequate services for the routine flights to Berlin prior to the Airlift, but there was now a requirement for a special weather service that could observe and forecast, as well as brief aircrews, on a 24-hour-day basis. In addition to the increase in traffic, the low operating minima involved special observations, special charts and special forecasts throughout the whole Airlift area. As the Airlift developed, Task Force planners began demanding weather forecasts over longer advance periods in an effort to determine their needs in terms of personnel and aircraft during the coming winter months. As a result, the 18th Weather Squadron was expanded to Group status in November 1948, which effectively meant that the Air Weather Service in Europe now had three squadrons: the 18th, serving the Airlift and Central European area, the 28th, serving the United Kingdom, and the 29th in Tripoli and Dharan. The squadrons were equipped with WB-29s.

By September 1948, the influx of USAF personnel to the Airlift theatre on temporary duty was being carried out on a regular basis, and the number of personnel assigned to the Airlift now stood at 1,320 officers and 3,605 airmen — figures that were to rise to 2,374 officers and 7,563 airmen by the end of the year. Many personnel were ordered to Airlift duty from theatres outside Europe on very short notice and in many cases this caused hardship, since officers and airmen were not given sufficient time to take care of personal affairs before proceeding overseas. Many came to Europe believing that their TDY would last only 45 days, and instead found themselves having to serve 90. Later in the Airlift, this period was extended to 180 days, and as a consequence a number of personnel had to be returned to their home stations prematurely to alleviate pressing emergencies, usually of a domestic nature.

On 16 December 1948 the C-54s of the 317th Troop Carrier Wing, which had been operating out of Wiesbaden, began moving to Celle in the British Zone. Some 2,000 German workers had been employed on the tremendous task of constructing the necessary operational facilities and housing. Eventually, Celle was to house 443 officers and 2,799 airmen, American and British. Meanwhile, as part of the USAF build-up in the United Kingdom, another British airfield had been allocated for use by Strategic Air Command. This was Sculthorpe, near Fakenham in Norfolk, which had been used by squadrons of the RAF's No 100 (Countermeasures) Group during the war before being closed for modernization in 1945. Its runways were lengthened and it was reopened in December 1948, ready for the eventual arrival — in February 1949 — of the 92nd Bomb Group with its B-29s.

Behind the scenes, vital decisions were also being taken which were to have a far-reaching effect on East-West relations. In the autumn of 1948, President Truman had initiated a crash programme to increase America's stockpile of atomic weapons. The Russians were undoubtedly aware of this, and the US monopoly on nuclear weapons, even though such weapons were not present in Europe, was a major factor in persuading the Soviet Government to refrain from taking full aggressive action to secure Berlin. It also, without doubt, spurred them to greater efforts in developing their own first-generation atomic weapons, and it was to come as a profound shock to the Western Allies when the Russians detonated their first nuclear device in 1949, years ahead of the predicted date. The age of deterrence was beginning, and Berlin was its cradle.

Chapter Five
Meanwhile, in Berlin ...

There was no relaxation in the principal Soviet weapon — intimidation — during those first months of the Berlin Airlift. The people on the receiving end were mostly Germans, but there were instances of British, American and French people suffering extreme harassment too. One man who experienced it, to his cost, was John Sims, a British Occupation officer, who was arrested by the Russians and accused of spying while he was investigating a hold-up of British-controlled barge traffic at Wittenberge on 14 July 1948. At 4.30 on that Wednesday afternoon he was taken before a Russian Major named Suev at Perleberg. Sims described what happened:

'Major Suev asked me if I was an American. I replied: "No. I live in London." The major remarked, "London, good place". At 9 pm I was made to lie in some stinking straw in a lorry while four Russian tommy-gunners stood guard over

Transport barges at a standstill on the River Elbe, viewed from an RAF Sunderland, after the Russians closed the access routes to Berlin.

me. Thursday, 3.30 am: At the Russian *Kommandatura* in Berlin, I was marched upstairs and handed over to some Russian soldiers. I had to turn out my pockets. Half an hour later I was put into a badly lit cell which was filthy, wet and stank. The bed comprised three wooden boards.

'Friday, 8.30 am. The Russian Commandant, after inspecting my cell, remarked, "It is good". I asked for my interpreter, but he shoved me away. 7 pm: a Russian Major did everything he could to humiliate me in front of some Russian soldiers.

'Saturday, 2.45 pm. A Russian soldier came into my cell with a lamb chop, potatoes, cabbage and brown bread. This compared with watery soup, brown bread and ersatz tea I had been offered on previous days. But I couldn't eat it, even though the Russian soldier tried to make me.'

After that, things happened quickly. At 3 pm Sims received a visit from the Russian Major, who remarked on how dirty the Englishman looked. The Russian got a clothes brush and insisted on having Sims brushed down. Five minutes later, the Russian read a long statement which purported to explain why Sims had been arrested, and asked if he agreed with it. Later, he discovered that the document was an order issued by Marshal Sokolovsky stating that any Briton found in the Soviet Zone without a Soviet inter-Zone pass would be arrested. At the time, sensing that the document was a preliminary to his release, Sims said that he did agree with it, although he had no idea what it was all about as it was in Russian. His intuition turned out to be correct; at 3.30 a British Army Captain arrived and escorted him back to the British Sector.

The American Commandant, Colonel (later Brigadier-General) Frank Howley was also the victim of harassment, although in his case it was psychological rather than physical. He would receive threats over the telephone from mysterious callers, and sometimes there would be no-one there at all when he lifted the receiver. At other times his doorbell would ring in the middle of the night, yet there would be no-one there. Despite these annoyances, the US Commandant refused to surround himself with armed guards, and his wife, showing considerable courage, insisted on staying in Berlin with their four children during Howley's tour of duty.

More serious, from the point of view of establishing and maintaining law and order in Berlin, was the growing Russian pressure on the *Magistrat*, the city administration. Up to mid-July 1948 travel between the respective sectors of the city was still relatively unrestricted, but then the Russians began to stage armed raids on the groups of black marketeers who were trading in the Potsdamer Platz, where the four sectors met, and there were some potentially dangerous confrontations between Soviet and American troops when the latter turned out to prevent the Russians from pursuing civilians who were seeking refuge in the American Sector. After that, the British and Americans erected steel barricades at the points where their sector boundaries began, and placed armed MPs as sentries. Across Berlin, the barriers were going up.

One constant thorn in the flesh of the *Magistrat* was Paul Markgraf, a former Nazi officer who had been converted to Communism during captivity in Russia

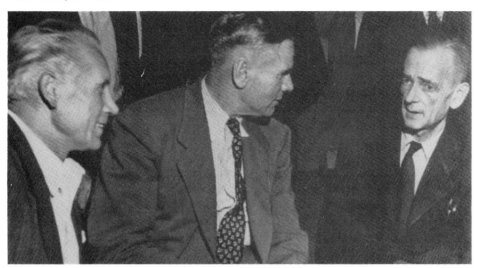

Members of Berlin's City Council in conference during the blockade.

and who had been appointed Chief of Police in Berlin by the Soviet Occupation authorities. In the last half of July, however, Markgraf overstepped even his considerable authority. As the start of a campaign to turn the Berlin police into an all-Communist force, he summarily dismissed 590 non-Communist officers. The reaction of the *Magistrat* was swift. Although Markgraf could not be sacked — that needed the agreeement of all four occupying powers — he could be suspended, and this is the action they took. Markgraf was replaced by a professional policeman, a Socialist named Johannes Stumm, who set up his HQ in West Berlin and invited volunteers to join him from the Soviet Sector. To the annoyance of the Russians many did, including a number of senior officers.

The Russians immediately embarked upon a campaign of reprisal; from that time on, any policeman from the western sectors who set foot in the eastern sector was liable to be arrested. Some were kidnapped, beaten up and even stabbed. Also, for the first time and in complete breach of the Berlin Air Safety regulations, the Russians sent formations of up to twenty fighters to circle the western sectors of the city, although this practice ceased when the senior British Air Officer in Berlin, Air Commodore Waite, made a strong protest.

Matters reached an ugly pitch in August, when the Russians — realizing that the city administration had overwhelmingly rejected all attempts at covert Communist domination — resorted to more direct means of attack. On 26 August, a crowd of 4,000, plied with drink and spearheaded by truckloads of young Communist supporters, marched on the Stathaus intent on disrupting the afternoon meeting of the Assembly. The latter had in fact been cancelled when word of what was about to happen filtered through, so the Communists were left to occupy an empty council chamber before eventually drifting off.

A Communist-organized crowd demonstrating outside Berlin's City Hall in 1948. The Russians failed to intimidate the city's civilian administration.

The next day the chamber was invaded again, this time by a smaller mob, and once again the meeting had to be called off. Then, on 6 September, 46 western sector police in plain clothes volunteered to protect the Stadthaus when another meeting of the Assembly was called; however, they could not prevent mobs of Communist 'action squads' from breaking into the building and taking over. Shortly afterwards, the building was invaded by 200 armed Communist police sent by Paul Markgraf, who combed the building for the western sector policemen. The latter sought refuge in the offices normally occupied by British, American and French liaison officers, but that did not save them from being dragged out, arrested and hauled off into the Soviet Sector under heavy guard. They were held until 22 October, when most were released on the eve of a United Nations Security Council meeting to discuss the Berlin crisis.

Meanwhile, the Berlin City Assembly had given up all hope of conducting its affairs in the Stadthaus, which stood in the Parochialstrasse, a street in the Bezirk Mitte of the Soviet Sector. From then on it gathered in the Schöneberg Town Hall, in the British Sector, and governed the western sectors only.

The action of the Communists provoked a furious reaction among Berliners. On 9 September, 300,000 of them crammed into the Platz der Republik, which marked the boundary between the British and Soviet Sectors, to voice their rage. It was the biggest voluntary mass meeting ever held in Germany — even Hitler's orchestrated rallies had never commanded a crowd this big. They listened to various speakers, who condemned the Communist policies, and the meeting stayed trouble-free until it began to break up. Then several thousand people, pouring through the Brandenburg Gate on their way home into the Soviet Sector, spontaneously began to stone a number of Soviet trucks carrying Communist police. Russian troops and police reinforcements were soon on the scene and, after shooting into the air, fired some shots into the crowd, fatally wounding a fifteen-year-old boy. Some youths climbed on top of the Brandenburg Gate and ripped down the Russian flag, which the crowd tore to pieces. More Russian troops arrived, firing their tommy-guns into the air, and a potentially explosive situation was averted by the timely arrival of some British Military Police, who positioned themselves between the crowd and the Russians. The latter ceased firing, and the crowd gradually dispersed. The toll was one killed (the fifteen-year-old) and 23 injured, mostly by thrown stones.

These incidents took place at a time when, in the eyes of the Western Allies, there appeared to be some hope that the Soviet blockade of Berlin might be lifted. On 26 July, the UK Foreign Minister, Ernest Bevin, had presided at the Foreign Office in London over a conference of US and British representatives to consider a joint reply to the latest Soviet Note on the Berlin crisis. The talks were attended by the US Ambassadors in London and Moscow, Lewis Douglas and General Bedell Smith, the British Ambassador in Moscow, Sir Maurice Peterson, Sir William Strang of the Foreign Office and Charles Bohlen of the US State Department. Two days later, it was announced that complete agreement had been reached in the London discussions on the form and method of the three-power reply to the USSR, and on the joint approach to be made by Britain, the USA and France in connection with the Berlin situation. That same day, Frank Roberts, Ernest Bevin's personal secretary, left for Moscow by air with General Bedell Smith; Roberts, who had been Chargé d'Affaires in Moscow during 1946-47, was chosen to act for Great Britain since Sir Maurice Peterson had returned home on sick leave and was not well enough to travel. They were joined in Moscow by the French Ambassador, Yves Chataigneau.

The next day the three Western representatives met Vyacheslav Molotov, the Soviet Foreign Minister, and requested a personal meeting with Marshal Stalin. This was held on 2 August, and a second meeting took place on the 23rd. Neither produced any result, with the exception that between 31 August and 7 September the military governors in Berlin met seven times and there were several meetings at a lower level during which experts discussed currency, trade and transport. All were inconclusive and ended in deadlock, but during that week reports reached Berlin that coal trains were waiting at Helmstedt for the signal to start the journey to Berlin, and the next day there were rumours that some had actually set out. But the rumours were unfounded, and gradually the air of optimism dissipated.

The Airlift went on, and in that summer weather the sight of the silvery transports descending on Berlin in an endless stream — like strings of pearls in the sky, as one Berliner described them — remained the principal attraction, not to mention reassurance. On Sundays, the banks of Lake Havel would be thick with picnic parties, watching the RAF's majestic Sunderland flying-boats touch down in their plumes of foam. It was times such as this that helped the Berliners to forget the monotonous diet, the lack of reliable news, the electricity shortage — and the knowledge that the summer warmth would soon give way to the first chills of autumn and then the misery of another austere winter.

The Berliners knew, now, that the Western Allies would not abandon them. They knew also that the transports could bring in sufficient food to meet their bare needs. The main concern, as the summer drew on, was to stockpile fuel for the winter, for the coal flown into the city was destined for industry, food production and hospitals. The Berlin suburbs were virtually stripped of dead wood, although citizens were forbidden to fell trees; it was something reminiscent of the mediaeval English law which forbade peasants to cut live firewood, but gave them the right to gather fallen sticks or to pull down dead branches with their billhooks or shepherd's crooks — a practice that gave rise to the old expression 'by hook or by crook'. Berliners could, however, get a permit to dig out the stumps of trees which had already been felled, although by way of payment they were required to fill in the holes where three other stumps had been. Combing the Berlin rubble was a much more satisfactory and less tiring way of finding combustible material, although it had its own hazards from dislodged and falling masonry.

With the cold coming on, a major concern was to ensure the safety of thousands of undernourished Berlin children, many of them orphans, and tuberculosis sufferers, and priority was given to flying out both. The USAF flew out 1,500 tuberculosis patients in the course of the Airlift, while the RAF and USAF together evacuated 15,426 children, most of them going to the British Zone. One RAF Dakota pilot, approaching Wunstorf with a planeload of kids, suddenly found himself with an unexpected problem when the aircraft went tail-heavy on the approach to land; it stayed tail-heavy, teetering just above the stall, despite full forward trim and much strenuous pushing. It turned out that the teenager in charge of the children had thought it a good idea for his charges to visit the lavatory in the tail of the aircraft before landing. The orderly queue was hurriedly moved forward again, and the trim retuned to normal just in time.

Mark Arnold-Forster, who was a journalist blockaded in Berlin in 1948, gives an excellent description of what Berliners had to endure in winter in his book *The Siege of Berlin.*

'The winter cold of 1948-49 was a severe experience. Berlin is a city of Central Europe. It lies in the plain of the Mark of Brandenburg. The ony windbreak between Berlin and Siberia is the Ural Mountains and the Polish frontier is only forty minutes' drive from Karlshorst in East Berlin. The nearest piece of sea, the Baltic, is not blessed by the Gulf Stream and much of it usually freezes over.

'The cold of the winter was made worse than it would otherwise have been by the weakening of those buildings which had not actually been destroyed. It is difficult to heat a house if the windows have been cracked and there is no glass with which to mend them. To withstand the cold the West Berliners received a weekly ration of coal which they were able to take home in their shopping bags but a shopping bag half-full of coal does not suffice to keep a family warm for a week when it is snowing . . .

'In spite of all these problems and privations no-one is known to have died of cold in West Berlin during the winter of 1948-49. Nor is it known that anyone died of hunger. Rations were short but they were dependable. The main deprivation, compared to what had gone before, was that it became difficult to obtain fresh vegetables from the Soviet Zone. In a modest way the Mark of

Brandenburg is a market-garden, brought to fruition by the Huguenots; it has always provided Berlin with fruit and vegetables, especially asparagus, and, above all, potatoes to which the Berliners are singularly addicted.

'Before the blockade began the West Berliners were able to draw on this, their traditional market-garden, for supplements to their meagre rations. Between 1945 and 1948 the start of the asparagus season in the Soviet Zone was greeted in West Berlin with the same sort of enthusiasm which, in France, celebrates the arrival of the first of the New Year's Beaujolais. The start of the strawberry season was a similar event. These happy anniversaries did not, however, survive during the blockade. West Berlin housewives, venturing into East Berlin to visit greengrocers (as they still then could) were harassed by the People's Police. The police would even confiscate potatoes.

'Of all the West Berliners the housewives were called upon to make the greatest sacrifice. What has often been forgotten is that during the blockade the grass was greener on the Eastern side. There were more vegetables. There was more food. There was more electric current. In the autumn of 1948 the East Germans and the Russians offered all West Berliners the chance to share in these comparative delights. West Berliners had the chance to take up East Berlin ration cards which were then more generous than those which were valid in the Western sectors. Out of 2.1 million West Berlin residents only 20,000 accepted the offer and many of them later rejected it and returned to the West. But the West Berlin housewife's main problems were to feed her family, to keep them warm, and to keep their clothes clean. It is a problem too familiar to bear repetition but in a situation in which power cuts prevail over the periods in which electricity is on the problem becomes appalling. Candles became pearls beyond price. So did vacuum flasks. Without their help it was impossible to keep coffee hot during a power cut. Without heat, also, there could be no laundry. Berlin housewives used to get up in the middle of the night in order to wash and iron their husbands' shirts during the period when the power was on. It is difficult to do all these awkward things and remain cheerful. Yet the Berlin housewives succeeded.'

The Americans and British joined forces to make the Christmas of 1948 a memorable one for as many families in Berlin as possible. The British ran their concerts at Gatow, but it was predictably the Americans who stole the show. In fact they had been stealing it for some time prior to Christmas, with an operation that became known as 'Little Vittles'.

It appears to have begun through the kindness of a MATS pilot called Lieutenant Gail S. Halverson, who took a walk through Berlin one day in the autumn of 1948. Halverson had been around most of the world since he became a transport pilot, and the thing that struck him most about the German children he met in the street was that, unlike their counterparts in Italy, Africa, Latin America and elsewhere, they did not beg for anything. Halverson, feeling sorry for them, told one group of children that if they congregated at the end of the Tempelhof runway the next day he would drop some gum and chocolate to them. They were there sure enough, and Halverson did as he had promised, bundling the sweets into handkerchiefs and arranging for his crew chief to drop them through the hatch.

Gradually, as the days went by, the word spread and the crowd of children at Tempelhof got bigger. Other pilots on Halverson's squadron joined in, and then 'Little Vittles' spread to other squadrons too. There was a sudden run on gum and chocolate at the PX on Rhein-Main and Wiesbaden as both air and ground crews made collections; all ranks joined forces in making parachutes out of handkerchiefs, old shirts, sheets and any other scraps of material. The Press got hold of the story, Halverson was flown back to the United States for a

Berlin children watch from the rubble of their city as US transport aircraft maintain the Air Bridge.

couple of days to appear on a national radio show, and as a result tons of gifts flooded into Rhein-Main from well-wishers back home. Every day, the sky over the cemetery next to Tempelhof, where the children gathered, would be filled at a certain time with hundreds of tiny parachutes, each carrying its package of sweets. The children never forgot who had started it all; they nicknamed Halverson *Der Schokoladeflieger* — The Chocolate Airman — and at Christmas 1948 he was showered with more than 4,000 cards and letters from them.

American writer Frank Donovan, who tells this rather touching story in his book *Bridge in the Sky*, adds:

'When school children were asked to draw pictures of the Airlift almost all of them showed Berliners participating in the Airlift in some way. One youngster drew a picture of a family, complete with cat and dog, standing on the roof of their house looking up at parachutes floating down from an Airlift plane above, each with an appropriate gift for a member of the family: a bone for the dog, a mouse for the cat, a toy train for the little boy, and a food package for Momma and Papa.'

So it was that the men of the Airlift captured the hearts of Berlin's children, and a lot of adult hearts too. Predictably, the Russians tried to make a propaganda exercise out of 'Little Vittles'; the Eastern Sector press lost no time in pointing out that the lack of respect shown by children running loose in a graveyard was another example of American barbarism. It was a miserable attempt to discredit a worthwhile cause, and it failed equally miserably. Sadly, luxury gifts reaching the Airlift bases in the Western Zones reached such proportions that a halt had to be called to 'Little Vittles' as an individual effort. Instead, the gifts were pooled and packed into bulk cargo to be flown into Berlin in the normal manner. But the citizens of Berlin received more necessary contributions in large quantities, too, as Frank Donovan recalls:

'Throughout West Germany a special two pfennig stamp was required in addition to the regular postage stamp, proceeds from the sale of which were used to buy supplies for Berlin. Later, special "Help Berlin" ten and twenty pfennig stamps were placed on sale for voluntary use. Citizens of Westphalia and Saxony went on a one-day fast and contributed the day's food ration, plus 100,000 tons of coal to Berlin. The city of Bremen donated twenty million cigarettes. Hamburg sent a collection of urgently needed medical supplies to which the Bavarian Red Cross added a ton of medicines. In Munich the Simpl Cabaret had a Berlin Night Benefit to support Berlin entertainers. Citizens of Westphalia also collected 10,000 candles which were flown to the blacked-out capital. Schleswig- Holstein sent two million pine tree seedlings to replace the trees that had been bombed or cut down in Berlin.'

The upkeep of morale was a key factor throughout the Berlin Blockade, and out of this realization was born RIAS — Radio in the American Sector — which, run jointly by US personnel and German broadcasters, became renowned for the quality of its programmes. Its first major task, as journalist Mark Arnold-Forster remembers, was to tell the truth clearly during the blockade and to make people laugh.

'On Christmas Day, 1948, when the outlook for West Berlin was about as black as it could be, RIAS launched a new programme which was to become a by-word not just in Berlin but throughout the Soviet Zone. Eight inspired entertainers, led by Günter Neumann, gave the first of 148 episodes of *Die Insulaner* (The Islanders). Their main theme, which they maintained until the end, was that for some reason they could not fully understand, Berlin was surrounded by water. Neumann's gifted collaborators — Tatjana Sais, Edith Schollwer, Bruno Fritz, Ilse Trautschold, Jo Furtner, Agnes Windeck and Ewald Wenck — were all Berliners or had become Berliners. Their humour was devastating. Their victims were everywhere. They persuaded cold and hungry Berliners to stop thinking for a while about the next meal or kilogramme of coal. And they made the Berliners laugh at everybody. They took the liberty (as it then was) of laughing at the occupying powers, Western as well as Russian. They laughed at the East German authorities and, above all, they made the Berliners laugh at themselves. Not many Germans have this gift — or not many had it in those days — but Günter Neumann did, so did *Die Insulaner*, and so — as matters turned out — did the Berliners themselves ... '

But for many Berliners, the big event of the winter of 1948 was a fairly regular allocation of potatoes — not in their natural form, but as 'POM', the dehydrated variety much used by the British armed forces. Many Berlin housewives who were unfamiliar with the substance expressed their amazement when POM, mixed with water, turned into a creamy substance that tasted very little like potatoes but made a nourishing soup when mixed with chopped vegetables. And they made humour out of that, too. With bitter memories of 1945, when an imperious wave of the hand and a harsh 'woman — come!' from an unshaven unwashed Russian soldier was the prelude to unspeakable humiliation and degradation, they said: 'Better POM than *Frau, komm!*'

On 26 December the Berlin Airlift completed its first six months of operations, during which period 96,640 flights — an average of 552 flights a day — had been made between the British and American Zones and the three airfields of the city. A total of 700,172 tons of food, coal, raw materials and manufactured goods had been brought into Berlin, an average of 3,800 tons a day. During this six-month period there had been seven fatal crashes involving US aircraft and two involving RAF aircraft, claiming the lives of seventeen American and nine British airmen. In the 24 hours ending at noon on 27 December the combined airlift achieved its second highest record by flying 6,430 tons of food and coal into Berlin in 749 flights, the record tonnage of 6,987 tons having been flown in on 18 September. The total mileage flown by Airlift aircraft during the six months was 34,410,000 miles (55,376,013 km).

And the end was by no means in sight.

Chapter Six
The civil Airlift

As the daily Airlift tonnage requirement grew, it was soon realized that sufficient military aircraft could not be spared to provide the necessary lifting capacity. For this reason, civilian aircraft were chartered to bridge the gap. Before this stage was reached, however, a need arose for specialized aircraft capable of carrying petrol, and as Flight Refuelling Ltd already had Lancastrian tankers in commission, three of them were chartered by the Air Ministry.

Flight Refuelling Ltd had a vast amount of experience in aerial tanker operations. The company had been founded in 1936 by the aviation pioneer Sir Alan Cobham, who had begun to practise flight refuelling as a science, rather than an air circus stunt, in 1933. Apart from Cobham, the other principal figure in these early experiments was Wing Commander H. Johnson, who had been chief pilot in Cobham's 'Flying Circus'. In 1933, he had flown a Handley Page W 10 from which Cobham flight-refuelled an Airspeed Courier. On 20 January 1938, Cobham had demonstrated the commercial possibilities of in-flight refuelling by transferring fuel from an Armstrong Whitworth AW23 bomber-transport — the sole prototype of which had been loaned to Flight Re-fuelling Ltd by the Air Ministry — to a C-class Empire flying boat of Imperial Airways.

During the war, with Wing Commander Johnson as his company's General Service Executive, Cobham had undertaken various flight refuelling projects on behalf of the Air Ministry and also for the United States Department of the Air Force. In May 1948, when the Berlin crisis was about to break, Flight Refuelling Ltd had just completed a series of winter trials with its Lancastrians on behalf of the Ministry of Civil Aviation, the idea being to use these aircraft to refuel Liberator transports of BOAC on their long-distance runs. When the Airlift began, the company was in the throes of a move to Tarrant Rushton, a deserted airfield in Dorset, and it was from there that Cobham offered his services to the Foreign Office.

The Avro 691 Lancastrian, a commercial conversion of the Lancaster bomber, was used by some companies — including Trans-Canada Airlines, BOAC and British South American Airways — as an interim airliner in the immediate post-war years, and was the first British commercial type physically capable of crossing the South Atlantic. By 1947-48, however, it had been relegated to hack transport work and the carriage of bulk liquids, particularly

milk and petroleum. The first flight by a Flight Refuelling Lancastrian on Airlift operations was made on 27 July 1948 by tanker G-AKDR (Captain D. Hanbury, DSO), which carried a load of petrol to Berlin from its home base of Tarrant Rushton, in Dorset. Operations were continuing from Bückeburg airfield on a temporary basis, and no special arrangements for liquid fuel loading or unloading were made at this time. No-one, then, could have foreseen the magnitude of the task that would have to be undertaken by the end of the year.

While this phase of the civil Airlift operation was in progress, discussions were being held in London between the Foreign Office, Air Ministry and Ministry of Civil Aviation on the further use of civil aircraft. The charter superintendent of British European Airways, Colonel G. Wharton, OBE, was called in as technical advisor in view of his knowledge of the charter market. As a result of these talks, the civil airlift came into being with a small fleet of ten Dakotas, which were to be based at Fassberg, and two Short Hythe flying boats, which were to operate from Finkenwerder on the Elbe. One Handley Page Halton and one Liberator were also chartered and based at Wunstorf alongside the RAF's Avro Yorks for a trial period, because doubts were expressed about their serviceability and loading facilities. The Halton's large ventral freight pannier, capable of holding 8,000 lb (3,629 kg), made the Halifax adaptation a relatively useful transport aircraft, but it required a special loading technique and the aircraft themselves had been heavily worked by their respective operators.

Owing to the number of separate companies now involved, it was also decided that BEA should provide liaison officers in Germany through whom the RAF could channel instructions to the operating companies, to deal with administrative problems and keep records on which payments to the companies could be based.

The Dakotas were provided by six charter companies: Air Contractors (G-AIWC, G-AIWD and G-AIWE), Air Transport (CI) (G-AJVZ), Kearsley Airways (G-AKAR and G-AKDT), Scottish Airlines (G-AGWS and G-AGZF), Trent Valley Aviation (G-AJPF) and Westminster Airways (G-AJAY). Later, Westminister added a second Dakota, G-AJAZ. Also at a later date, more civilian Dakotas were provided by British Nederland Air Services (G-AJX), British Overseas Airways Corporation (G-AGIZ, G-AGNG and G-AGNK), Ciros Aviation (G-AIJD and G-AKJN), Hornton Airways (G-AKLL) and Sivewright Airways (G-AKAY). The Short Hythes were supplied by Aquila

Top left *Lancasters of Flight Refuelling Ltd pictured before conversion to Lancastrian standard. The aircraft nearest the camera, G-AHJU, carried nearly 2,500 tons of liquid fuel into Berlin.*

Above left *Tanking up Flight Refuelling's Lancastrians prior to a flight to Berlin.*

Left *A Lancastrian tanker en route to Berlin over the mist-shrouded landscape of northern Germany.*

Airways, a new company formed at a time when BOAC and other world airlines had decided that there was no future in flying boats, while the Halton came from Bond Air Services and the Liberator (*G-AHDY*) was provided by Scottish Airlines.

For most of these companies, formed in the early post-war years by enthusiastic young men who had survived the war and who had scraped together every penny to purchase surplus transport aircraft, the Berlin Airlift was to be their heyday and also their swansong. Most of those companies named above did not survive beyond the early 1950s.

Overall direction was entrusted to BEA's general manager in Germany, E.P. Whitfield, as an additional commitment to his duties as the commercial manager of the Corporation in this territory.

Warning of the arrival of the civilian aircraft in Germany, scheduled for 4 August 1948, was not received until the 1st, but in spite of this short notice the necessary arrangements were made for the first sorties to take place on the following day. The first sortie was flown at night by Halton *G-AIOI* (Captain Treen) of Bond Air Services, which landed at Gatow at 03:10 local time. This aircraft carried out five return flights between Wunstorf and Berlin in the first 24 hours of operations, which produced a total of 33 sorties from the civil side.

It was inevitable, in view of the way in which the civil air reinforcements were rushed into action on the Airlift, that these early operators should run into many difficulties. There was no time to send out advance parties to explore what facilities were available in Germany, to obtain a full briefing on operational procedures, wireless frequencies, loading arrangements and so on, or to set up a proper maintenance organization. It speaks well for the initiative and resource of the operators that, although their aircraft only arrived at their base in Germany on the evening of the 4th, they were able to commence operations without any delay or fuss the next morning. Difficulties had to be overcome, and strenuous efforts were made, not only by the operators themselves, but also by the RAF, who showed themselves always ready to give prompt and immediate assistance. As an example, on the eve of the start of the civil operation, despatch riders had to be sent to RAF stations in Germany to obtain radio crystals for the civil aircraft sets, so that they could be tuned to the special radio frequencies used on 'Plainfare'. Then, at the initial conference at Fassberg, the Army asked that the civil Dakotas carry the same standard payload of 7,480 lb (3,393 kg) as the similar RAF type. As this weight was in excess of the 6,000 lb (2,722 kg) allowed by the civil aircraft's Certificate of Airworthiness, arrangements had to be speedily improved for special loads to be prepared for the civilians. Applications were immediately made to the Air Registration Board for the standard load to be carried, but clearance was not received until 15 August.

A further difficulty was that the payloads of individual aircraft varied, as some companies had not fully stripped the interiors of passenger furnishings and other unnecessary dead weight. This problem was also solved by 16 August, when all civilian Dakotas began operating with the 7,480 lb (3,393 kg) payload. Accommodation, hangar, transport and workshop facilities also presented difficult problems which had to be ironed out with the full co-operation of the RAF. Unfortunately, none of the operating companies had brought with them responsible administrative personnel, and the position at the time was that each unit was under the control of the senior captain, who in fact was fully engaged on flying duties. This not only meant that every point, even of minor detail, had to be taken up with the company's head office in London, which was a slow and cumbersome method, but also that the burden placed on the BEA liaison officers was considerably greater than had at first been envisaged. Moreover, as only two liaison officers had been sent to each base and were required to cover a 24-hour operation, these men were considerably overworked and deserved every praise for the way in which they stood up to the continual pressure of those early months.

To complicate matters still further, the extent to which RAF assistance could be invoked was not clearly defined, but this drawback was largely offset by the willingness of all members of the Service to give every help in their power. Neither was there in the contract any clear-cut definition of the regularity of operational effort required from each company, nor stipulation made of the number of aircrew, maintenance personnel or range of spares to be provided. All these important factors were left mainly to the discretion of the individual operator, who was therefore in a position to assess whether the provision of more adequate resources of manpower and material would provide a greater financial return when balanced against capital outlay. In making a decision, he had to take into account the insecurity of his position on the Airlift, and there can be no doubt that the one week's cancellation clause in the contract was a determining factor which made any substantial expenditure a very hazardous commercial risk.

The companies themselves differed considerably in material resources, as well as in personnel strength, operating standards and technical efficiency. The sporadic nature of their business before the Airlift, which was subject to the fluctuations of the air charter market, made them at the start ill-equipped and inexperienced in sustained operations of high intensity in all weathers. As they expanded their aircraft strength, so the burden on their base facilities in the United Kingdom was overtaxed, and they experienced the greatest difficulty in finding enough trained aircrew with recent flying experience on the types operated.

Similarly, the supply of spare parts, the consumption of which rose steeply with the intensity of flying, was a source of constant anxiety, particularly with the Dakota companies operating American equipment. Most of these problems haunted the civil Airlift almost to the very end, but to an ever-decreasing degree, and were fortunately never to loom as large again as they did in the first three months of operations. In the early phase, they were brought into sharp relief because of haphazard planning on the civil side, and this seemed almost insurmountable. However, the fact remains that they were overcome, and by improvization and almost superhuman efforts on the part of the aircrew and

Lancastrian tankers of Flight Refuelling Ltd on the flight line at Wunstorf.

ground personnel, a highly intensive if somewhat irregular effort was maintained. This was largely due to the rumours which were current during the whole of August 1948 that the Airlift was coming to an end, and as far as the Dakotas were concerned these rumours were strengthened by the decision to move USAF C-54s to Fassberg.

Earlier in the month, on the 8th, Flight Refuelling Ltd were moved from Bückeburg to Wunstorf, where the Lancastrians joined the solitary Halton. The latter type had now proved itself satisfactory; although it was awkward to load, more aircraft of this type were ordered. On the other hand, the Liberator was withdrawn, as it had not produced a high enough standard of serviceability. Finally, on 28 August, the civil Dakotas joined their RAF counterparts at Lübeck. The move of the Dakotas temporarily ended rumours of their withdrawal, and the companies began to plan ahead with more confidence. This was an advantage which could be offset against the disruption caused by the move and the fact that the limited facilities at Lübeck were so overstrained by the sudden arrival of the civil unit that flying had to be restricted to daytime only for the first fortnight. Although this meant a loss of revenue to the owners, it turned out to be a blessing in disguise, as it gave the hard-worked crews a chance to rest and recoup, and the companies themselves an opportunity to organize their maintenance setup in Germany.

While the civil Airlift had been experiencing all these teething troubles at Fassberg and Lübeck, and to a lesser degree at Wunstorf, the flying boat operation at Finkenwerder was proceeding smoothly. As there were no night landing facilities on either the Havel or the Elbe, it had the advantage of being a purely daylight operation, and the attendant problems were correspondingly simple. The civil Hythes of Aquila Airways were manned by recently-demobilized ex-Coastal Command crews who knew many of the Service personnel at the base, and this fostered a spirit of good comradeship and keen rivalry between them. Excellent aircrew morale and good serviceability produced a steady three sorties a day from the two flying boats in the hours available for operations. Every effort was made by this company to increase their payload, which improved from 9,982 lb (4,528 kg) at the start to 10,900 lb (4,944 kg) by the end of August, and about 12,400 lb (5,625 kg) by the end of October.

With the approach of autumn, it became probable that the Russians intended to maintain the blockade throughout the winter months, and plans were made for a considerable expansion of the civil fleet. The dwindling stocks of liquid fuel in Berlin were also causing anxiety, and the assembly of an adequate tanker force was clearly becoming a matter or urgent necessity. A survey of all available charter aircraft in the UK was undertaken by BEA and a series of conferences held in London to decide on the most suitable types. The main consideration was to replace the lighter load carriers with heavy four-engined aircraft. Unfortunately there was not a great deal of choice open, and in the main it narrowed down to the Halton, which was the only large aircraft used in any quantity by the charter companies.

Although the Halton had given sterling service in the past it was now obsolete, and some of the aircraft actually used were of an age when, under different circumstances, they would have been retired. In addition, the unfortunate accidents involving Avro Tudors of British South American Airways, two of which disappeared under mysterious circumstances, had led to the grounding of these large aircraft as far as passenger flying was concerned and their relegation to freight duties, which meant that they were available for the Airlift. Being new machines, with ample stores backing, they were to prove an invaluable asset to the operation.

The first Tudor to join the Airlift was a Mk II, G-AGRY, which was operated by Air Vice-Marshal D.C.T. Bennett's newly-formed Airflight Company. This aircraft arrived at Gatow on 3 September, carrying a load of 20,000 lb (9,072 kg). Later in the month, BSAA began operations from Wunstorf with two Tudor Mk I freighters. Additional reinforcements also arrived at Wunstorf in September in the shape of two Halton freighters of Skyflight, two Wayfarers of Silver City and two Vikings of Trans-World Charter. The Wayfarer was the passenger version of the Bristol Freighter, and was used on the lift as a stopgap

Avro Tudor G-AGRY of Air Vice-Marshal Don Bennett's Airflight Company. This aircraft was the first Tudor to join the Airlift, making its initial trip to Gatow on 3 September 1948.

until the latter type could be made available. The Bristol Freighter was required to transport awkward loads such as cars, snowploughs and rolls of newsprint; its large loading doors at the front of the aircraft, and substantial internal capacity, made it very useful for this type of cargo.

Now that winter was approaching, the months of October and November 1948 saw a considerable influx of British and American military aircraft, and brought fresh difficulties for the civil Airlift. To absorb these reinforcements, a further redeployment of the civil fleet became necessary; although unavoidable, this happened at an awkward time, just as plans were being made to replace the lighter transport types with heavier aircraft. Every effort was made to keep the rate of flying as high as possible, but some inevitable loss of tonnage was experienced. To conform to the new pattern, the civil Dakotas were again moved on 6 October from Lübeck to Fühlsbüttel, Hamburg's civil airport, which now became a 'Plainfare' base. As this move was undertaken at short notice a great strain was placed on the airfield's resources, for there was not enough warning to prepare adequate accommodation or provide the necessary technical facilities. Great difficulty was experienced in persuading the aircrew to accept the quarters provided, even as a stop-gap.

As this was the third move in two months for the Dakota operators, their irritation was perhaps understandable. However, within a week the situation had improved with the billeting of the aircrew in a comfortable Hamburg hotel, and the opening of an engineer's mess at Fühlsbüttel. After this, the daily flying effort steadily improved. Work on improving the airfield facilities at Fühlsbüttel was also in progress, including the construction of a new 5,850 ft (1,783 m) concrete runway. This was laid parallel to the existing 4,800 ft (1,463 m) PSP strip, and building work proceeded at such a rapid rate that the new runway was ready for use on 21 December 1948. In addition, a large and well-illuminated tarmac loading apron was built and a new system of airfield lighting installed on the pattern of the installations at Wunstorf and Gatow, consisting of an approach path 3,000 ft (914 m) long, with white lights spaced every 100 ft (30.5 m) from the end of the runway and intersected every 600 ft (183 m) by a crossbar of sodium lights. The downwind end of the runway was marked by a green threshold bar, and the runway itself was defined by white contact lights on each side.

The Fühlsbüttel installation also included an experimental refinement in the form of a line of green lights down the runway centreline, and this was found extremely useful to pilots in checking incipient swings during night take-offs with a heavily-laden aircraft. Nevertheless, although the lighting system provided a useful visual landing aid in bad visibility, it was by no means a substitute for the normal blind approach aids. The lack of GCA at Fühlsbüttel was a serious drawback in bad weather, particularly as the alternative — a BABS beacon — was out of action for the greater part of the operation from this base, its beam being badly affected by the use of the construction equipment on the airfield.

The civil Dakotas at Fühlsbüttel continued to increase in number, but soon after the arrival of three BOAC Dakotas on 20 October their sorties were restricted owing to congestion at Gatow, and they were finally withdrawn

Above left *Bristol Freighters proved a great asset on the Berlin Airlift, carrying bulky cargoes to and from the beleaguered city.*

Right and below *Handley Page Halifax C VIII transport conversions of the famous bomber. After the war, 147 Halifaxes appeared on the British civil register, and many were converted to Haltons with the addition of a ventral freight pannier. A large fleet of these aircraft took part in the Berlin Airlift.*

between 10 and 23 November. In the previous month, the contract for Skyflight's Haltons was cancelled as the results achieved by this company had proven unsatisfactory, World Air Freight joined the Airlift on 6 October with one Halton, and this became the first civilian aircraft to be written off when, two days later, it broke its back following a swing on take-off at Gatow.

Further reinforcements were provided by Bond Air Services, who by this time had increased their committment to four aircraft; Eagle Aviation, with two Halifax transport conversions; and a Bristol Freighter from Airwork. They were joined by three Halton freighters of Lancashire Aircraft Corporation on 16 October, and by a Halton tanker of this Company on 30 October. In the meantime, Airflight had received a second Tudor Mk V, and both aircraft had been converted to tankers.

The Lancashire Aircraft Corporation's personnel, both flying and ground, were perhaps typical of all those who took part in the civil Airlift. Captain Dennis Richards, who opened the Corporation's Airlift activity on 16 October, was to make 229 flights to Berlin; the other two Halton pilots, Captains Nash and Franks, were to make the trip 222 and 216 times respectively. At Schleswigland, the corporation's Chief Engineer was L.D. Chapman, with Captain Marshall as Flight Captain. Each aircraft carried a crew of four — captain, navigating officer, radio officer and engineer officer — and twenty such crews were ultimately to be involved in the operation.

At Bovingdon, the corporation's base in Hertfordshire, the two principals were Captain Wallace Lashbrook, DFC, AFC, DFM, who was Chief Pilot and Operations Manager, and Mr Douglas R. Morgan, ARAeS, the Technical Manager. Thirty-six-year- old Captain Lashbrook had a distinguished career in the Royal Air Force (like many other Airlift captains) before joining Lancashire Aircraft Corporation in 1947. Halton apprentices have long been recognized as providing the RAF with some of its most outstanding officers, and it was at Halton that Captain Lashbrook received the thorough training which, combined with his own personality, led to rapid advancement. Gaining his 'wings' in 1936, he spent three years during the war as a bomber pilot operating over Germany and Italy. Promoted Squadron Leader in 1942, he was shot down in the following year, but evaded capture and eventually found his way home via Gibraltar after nine weeks of slogging over the Pyrenees. At the time of the Airlift, Captain Lashbrook had flown over 120 aircraft types.

Douglas Morgan, Lancashire's Technical Manager, received his basic training in the motor industry before joining the RAF at the outbreak of war. He served as an engineer during the Battle of Britain, then moved to No 4 Group Bomber Command, where he was mentioned in despatches and later commissioned in the Engineer Branch. During the period of the Airlift, Morgan and his staff worked at constant high pressure; in under four months they carried out nearly eighty inspections, some majors, fifty engine changes and eight complete C of A overhauls. The engineering branch at Bovingdon had to be capable of carrying out four 'Check Twos' (an inspection after 120 hours' flying) and six engine changes per week.

A booklet produced by the Lancashire Aircraft Corporation, produced at the close of the Airlift, gives an interesting glimpse into a typical civilian flight to the city, together with R/T procedures.

'We will assume that the flight is scheduled to take off from Schleswigland airfield at 04.30. This means an early night and a call at 02.30. Schleswigland is some seven miles from the barracks in Schleswig town, and the first stop is at the airfield buffet, where meals are served "round the clock" 24 hours a day, for breakfast. After the meal, to the Briefing Room to check the weather and get any relevant information concerning the route. The whole secret of the success of the Berlin Airlift is extreme accuracy in timing and navigation. The aircraft based in Northern Germany, ie at Schleswigland and Hamburg, fly to Berlin and leave it by the Northern corridor, running through the Russian Zone of Germany. This corridor is only twenty miles [32 km] wide, therefore the most accurate navigation is essential, especially in bad visibility, to maintain correct height and position, and to avoid collision with other aircraft. Aircraft *to* Berlin keep to the southern side of the corridor, aircraft *from* Berlin keep to the northern side.

'In the briefing room the navigator collects a slip of paper giving the aircraft identification letters, time to start engines, time to taxi out, time for take-off, time on turning points and over Frohnau Beacon. It is the Frohnau Beacon that provides the magic of the Airlift. As already explained, accurate navigation and precise timing alone enable an operation of the intensity of "Plainfare" to succeed. But, when flying in cloud for over an hour with no sight of anything on which to check actual physical position and when an alteration in wind velocity of a quarter of a mile per hour can do the damage, something more than chronometer and chart is needed. Working through an illuminated dial in the navigator's compartment, the beacon supplies that positive information, by radar, which enables the aircraft's position to be pinpointed, and gives the information over a sufficiently long period to allow the timing of the beacon itself to be accurate.

'To return to our journey — the crew are now in position, all hatches are closed, instruments are checked, and all is ready for "start up" time.

'At 04.20 the Captain calls: "All clear — OK to start up." The Engineer Officer primes the engines, and in rapid succession the four motors, each of 1,700 hp, turn slowly and spring to life. From then on, conversation between crew members is confined to intercom, while contact with the outside world is maintained by the Wireless Officer, via morse key, and by the Captain through his radio telephone.

'In the following paragraphs, italics denote radio telephone and intercom speech.

'Engineer Officer: (To Captain on intercom) *Temperature and pressure correct, ready for taxying.*

'Captain: *Schleswig Tower, Halifax HY, taxi clearance.*' [Note: crews habitually referred to the aircraft as the Halifax, rather than by the more correct name of Halton.]

'Schleswig Tower: *Halifax HY clear to taxi; runway two six, Queen Nan How one zero zero six.*' [QNH — altimeter setting above sea level — 1,006 millibars.]

'Captain: *Halifax HY, Roger.*

'The brakes are released and the thirty-ton aircraft moves forward under the compulsion of open throttles. Coming to a standstill again near the end of the runway, each engine in turn is opened wide, ignition switches are tested, propeller settings tried out, and the multifarious dials and levers checked. Meantime, the aircraft ahead takes off at its appointed time.

'Captain: *Schleswig Tower, Halifax HY, runway clearance.*

'Schleswig Tower: *Halifax HY, clear to take off, wind two six zero degrees one-five knots.*

'Now the heavily-laden aeroplane starts to move again as it swings on to the downwind end of the runway in use. Gathering speed, the tail lifts clear of the ground. The gradual lessening of weight on the giant mainwheel tyres can be seen until finally the huge structure is fully airborne, at home once more in its own element, as the next aircraft to take off gets ready to follow on the runway. Climbing steadily to the allotted height, and turning left into the circuit of the aerodrome, Halifax HY steadies on its first course.

'Now the navigator takes over. When the ground is visible in daytime, course is altered as necessary. But at night or in bad weather — often the entire route is flown in cloud and rain — course pre-computed on known or estimated winds are passed to the Captain. Before reaching the final check of Frohnau Beacon, there are two major alterations of course in order to get to, and fly along the air corridor.

'Captain: *Schleswig Approach, Halifax HY, first turning point ten seconds late.*

'Schleswig Approach: *Halifax HY, Roger.*

'Navigator: (To Captain on intercom) *New course one five zero degrees true. Increase speed to one six zero knots.*

'Captain: (To Navigator on intercom) *Roger.* (To Engineer on intercom) *1950 revs please.*

'Engineer Officer: (To Captain on intercom) *1950 Roger.*

'The flight proceeds in its own world of grey, enveloping cloud, bursts of rain obscuring the windscreen from time to time. The second turning point is reached thirty seconds late, and speed is once more slightly increased. At twenty miles from Frohnau Beacon, having gradually regained time and position, the Captain reports, giving his height and stating his cargo — in this case diesel oil.

'Meanwhile at Tegel, the Berlin airport used by the northern operators, the twenty miles message is received. On the graduated surface of the radar screen in the control tower, the aircraft arriving and leaving are followed as moving dots. Each aircraft must be identified, so HY is ordered to steer 45 degrees for thirty seconds so that positive identification may be made. Dead on time, HY reports over the Frohnau Beacon. From then on, instructions are passed by control to bring HY safely to the end of the landing runway at Tegel.

'HY: *Tegel Approach, Halifax HY over Frohnau at one point five* [1,500 ft/ 457 m].

An Avro York of Skyways, as used on the Berlin Airlift. Oddly enough, the aircraft carries no visible civil registration.

'Tegel Approach: *Roger HY, change to* 117.9 *m/cs, call Corkscrew* [GCA Control].

'HY: *Corkscrew Control, Halifax HY leaving Frohnau.*

'Corkscrew: *Roger HY, steer two six zero degrees at one point five, how do you read me?*

HY: *Read you loud and clear. Roger.*

'Corkscrew: *HY, you are now five and a half miles* [8.85 km] *north-west of the field, visibility one mile* [1.6 km], *light rain, wind south-south-east at ten, eight-eighths cloud 500 ft* [152 m].

'HY: *Roger.*

'Corkscrew: *HY, turn left, steer one eight zero degrees. Let down to one point two. Do your cockpit check for landing.*

'HY: *Roger.*

'Corkscrew: *HY, you are now on the base leg at one point two, turn left on to one zero zero degrees. Call your final controller on* 106.38.

'HY: *Roger. Hello, Final Controller, Halifax HY.*

'Final Controller: *HY, Final Controller, how do you read?*

'HY: *Loud and clear, out.*

'Controller: *Roger HY. If you do not hear me for more than five seconds, climb to 800 ft* [244 m], *home to Frohnau Beacon, call Tower for further instructions.*

'HY: *Roger.*

'Controller: *HY, do not answer any further instructions. Turn further left to zero nine five degrees, let down to 800 ft* [244 m]. *Your landing gear should be down and locked. Maintain 800 ft. You are approaching the centreline. Make final flap settings before reaching the glide path. Turn further left on to zero nine zero degrees. You are now on the glide path, start rate of descent of 650 feet per minute* [198 m per minute]. *Turn right two degrees on to zero nine two degrees. You are on the glide path, you are a little to the left of the centre line. You are coming below the glide path, decrease your rate of descent. You are on the centre line, steer left on to zero nine zero degrees. You are on the glide path, range one mile. Rate of descent is now very good, you are on the centre line, approaching the end of the runway. You are on the glide path, the runway is dead ahead. You are one-quarter mile [402 m] from the runway, take over visually and land ahead. Corkscrew out.*

'From now on, the landing is completed visually in the normal manner. HY rolls to walking pace, and turns off the runway.

'HY: *Tegel Tower, HY clear of runway.*

'Tegel Tower: *Roger HY, thank you.*

'Another seven tons of fuel oil has reached beleaguered Berlin.'

On 11 November 1948 the civil Airlift completed its first 100 days of operations, during which period it had carried 18,585 short tons in the course of 3,944 sorties. The second phase of operations, which lasted from 12 November 1948 to 19 February 1949, began with another major deployment of the civil fleet. The Haltons were moved out of Wunstorf to make room for three Avro Yorks of Skyways, which joined the lift on 16 November, and also for the anticipated arrival of BSAA's Tudor tankers. Bond Air Services and Eagle Aviation moved their freighters to Fühlsbüttel between 14 and 20 November, and Lancashire Aircraft Corporation moved their Haltons to Schleswigland on the 24th. With the withdrawal of the Vikings and Wayfarers during the same period, Wunstorf became exclusively an Avro base for Tudors, Lancastrians and Yorks.

Schleswigland opened for operations on 25 November with a combined force of RAF Hastings and civilian Haltons. It was a large airfield, with two excellent runways, but operations were handicapped by three major factors. Firstly, as the airfield was situated on the Baltic coast, it suffered particularly in the winter from low stratus and sea mist. Secondly, it was the most distant of the civil bases from Berlin, and during the first seven weeks of operation the route laid down meant an average flying time for the journey of three and a quarter to three and a half hours, compared with Hamburg's two hours and Wunstorf's two and a half hours. This meant that in forty sorties, a Schleswig-based aircraft completed fifty hours' more flying than one from Hamburg, and thirty hours more than one from Wunstorf. As the flying times from the latter bases made it practicable for aircraft operating from them to make a sortie every four hours, the longer flight from Schleswigland inevitably reduced their utilization rate. Moreover, the 6,000 ft (1,829 m) operating height laid down created serious problems for the Haltons, which were not equipped with proper wing de-icing equipment, and as the regulations prohibited a captain from altering his height, he was naturally reluctant to undertake a flight if a high icing index was forecast.

Allied to this was the problem of low temperatures on the ground. Of necessity the aircraft had to be parked in the open, it took half an hour to defrost them before starting up, and ice would sometimes have begun to form again by the time the aircraft were lined up for take-off. On one occasion, Captain Richards of Lancashire Aircraft Corporation accumulated so much ice on climbing to his operation height of 6,000 ft (1,829 m) that his aircraft dropped nearly 3,000 ft (914 m) before he could regain control and return to base.

Right *German workers loading sacks of coal on to a Hastings C Mk I at Schleswigland.*
Below *A German labour gang extending the facilities at Schleswigland during the Airlift, with Hastings of RAF Transport Command in the background.*
Bottom *Hastings taxying past German workmen constructing a new hardstanding at Schleswigland.*

The third main difficulty at Schleswigland was a shortage of hangar space, with only the smaller of the two existing hangars allocated for civil use. This had a serious effect on maintenance, since it was impossible for men to work out of doors for more than twenty minutes at a time before their hands became numb and useless. In December 1948 the civil Airlift as a whole was faced with an even more serious problem. A directive from HQ 46 Group, dated 17 December, laid down that British aircraft not fitted with Rebecca could only fly in VFR conditions. At this time of the year, the chances of finding VFR conditions at the operating height along the whole of the route to Berlin were remote, and neither the Haltons nor the Bristol Freighters were equipped with this essential radio aid.

The necessity for equipping the civilian aircraft with Rebecca had been foreseen, and the problem was referred to London on 13 August 1948 in the following words:

'For obvious reasons, it is essential that the civilian aircraft should be equipped with the same navigational aid, Rebecca, as the other aircraft flying at the same altitude in the traffic flow. Arrangements will have to be made to fit this equipment in the UK, as lack of technical personnel will make it impossible for the RAF to equip the whole fleet out here. In anticipation, I recommend that the opportunity should be taken to carry out this work as aircraft return to the UK for major checks.'

No immediate action was taken on this advice, because at the time the civil airlift was regarded as a stopgap. The problem was repeatedly raised in the early autumn, and finally an urgent warning was given at a conference in London on 14 October that unless immediate action was taken, the civil fleet would be grounded in less than two months. The Foreign Office then approached the Air Ministry, and by the end of the month agreement was reached that Rebecca Mk II sets would be supplied from RAF sources. Twenty-six sets were ordered, but then more difficulties arose. It took some time to negotiate the financial side of the transaction and to find out where the spare sets were located. It was not until early in December that sixteen were found at No 14 Maintenance Unit, near Carlisle. Most of them were unserviceable, and it was even necessary to manufacture some of the spare parts needed to repair them.

A further 28 sets were ordered in the middle of December, but it was not until 13 January 1949 that all the Haltons were equipped. In the meantime, the RAF in Germany arranged a series of lectures to instruct civilian aircrew in the use of Rebecca equipment. Fortunately, all the civil Avro aircraft at Wunstorf carried Rebecca as part of their normal equipment, and during this four-week period they were able to offset the serious loss of tonnage caused by the frequent cancellations of the Schleswigland and Fuhlsbüttel groups.

This loss was further aggravated by the need to withdraw a number of aircraft from active operations for fitting Rebecca, and also for converting them into tankers. Furthermore, the delay in supplying Rebecca had serious repercussions on the conversion programme, as it had been the intention that all sets should be fitted before work was due to start on converting the aircraft to

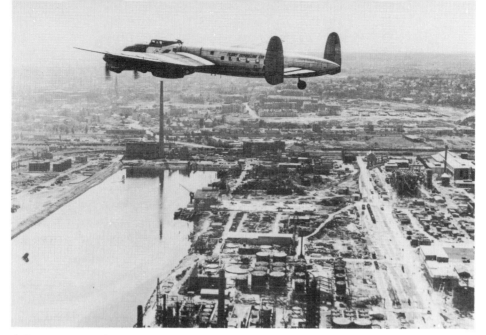

A Lancastrian tanker in flight over Berlin, 1949. Four years after the war, the bomb damage has been largely repaired.

tankers. As it was, towards the end of December the hangars and workshops of the home bases of the Halton companies were so congested with aircraft being fitted with Rebecca that the tanker conversion work had to be delayed until January. The result was that between mid-December and the end of January, the forecast daily rate of practically every civil reinforcement had to be put back on an average of two or three weeks.

This delay in the reinforcement of the tanker fleet was particularly serious, because by the end of 1948 the liquid fuel stocks in Berlin were practically exhausted, and from 1 January the city became dependent on airborne supplies carried entirely by the civil airlift. A daily target of 220 tons had been set, but because of the delays an average of only 148 tons was achieved. To fulfil the task, a fleet of 31 tankers had been planned for 1 January 1949, but on that day the actual strength was only eleven aircraft, increasing to twenty on the 14th. However, the tanker force was still four aircraft below strength at the end of the month.

Coupled with the delays in the conversions of the Haltons, a further disappointment had arisen in the full deployment of BSAA's Tudors. This was caused by the length of time taken to convert them from the passenger role to tankers. Five Tudor Mk V aircraft were scheduled to begin operations on 1 January, but only three were in commission on the 7th, and the other two did not arrive until 2 and 14 February respectively.

To provide crews for these aircraft, one of BSAA's Tudor Mk I aircraft had been withdrawn from the Airlift at the end of November 1948 for training purposes. In addition, Flight Refuelling had now increased their unit to seven Lancastrians, Skyways had brought in two Lancastrian tankers in addition to their three Yorks, and British American Air Services — a new company on the

Airlift — had positioned two Halton tankers at Schleswigland, Westminster one Halton on 20 January, and finally Lancashire Aircraft Corporation increased their commitment to ten tankers during the month. The composition of the tanker force at the end of January was therefore five Tudors, nine Lancastrians and thirteen Haltons, making 27 aircraft in all. In addition there were seventeen freighters, giving a total strength of 44 civilian aircraft.

With the increased number of tankers operating, the liquid fuel loading arrangements at Wunstorf and Schleswigland became sorely taxed. The system at Wunstorf was to fill road bowsers from a cistern wagon positioned at the rail spur on the airfield with the right quantity of fuel required for a particular aircraft. In the case of an uneven amount — 2,100 gallons (9,547 litres), for example — two bowsers had to be used, one receiving 1,000 gallons (4,546 litres) and the other 1,100 gallons (5,000 litres). The load was measured by means of a graduated dipstick on the boswer, which was then driven to the aircraft and pumped dry through flexible hoses by a portable pump, powered by an internal combustion engine. The system was operated by Army personnel of No 1 RASC Unit, Wunstorf, and was intended as a stopgap until a permanent underground installation could be built. By this method, it took forty minutes to load 2,100 gallons of diesel oil into a Tudor aircraft, which was considered adequate for normal purposes, although the time involved did not allow any margin for breakdowns. There were plenty of these, for the pumping equipment was not designed for such a heavy task. In the period 21 January- 21 April, there were fifty instances when aircraft were not fuelled within the forty minutes allowed, and as a result sorties were lost as aircraft could not make their beacon times. However, during the same period 2,827 tanker sorties were flown from Wunstorf, so that the loss of fifty represented only 1.8 per cent.

At Schleswigland, a fixed underground system was already installed, originally for the German night fighters which had been based there during the war. There were eighteen refuelling bays, supplied by six pumps fed from ten tanks. However, the pumps did not operate at the same rate, and loading was retarded by the action of flow meters fitted into the system. Nevertheless, the meters were a distinct advantage, as they would automatically cut out when the correct preselected load had been delivered. Two quick turn-round bays were improvized by Major Craig, commanding the RASC detachment at Schleswigland, by coupling two bays together so that the delivery force of two pumps could be applied to each bay. The result was that the fuelling time for a Halton was cut down from 20-25 minutes to 12-14 minutes, and the quick turnround available made it possible for extra sorties to be flown.

At the Berlin end, during the summer of 1948, there were available at Gatow two gasoline tanks with a capacity of 11,000 gallons (50,006 litres) each. Since both filler necks for these tanks lay in the same pit, it was not possible to empty more than two tankers at a time, and so plans were drawn up for the erection of new storage facilities. Construction work was started by the RAF at the end of September 1948 and completed in March 1949, five large underground tanks being built and connected to eighteen defuelling points. The latter were distributed around the perimeter of a circular island in the middle of the tarmac apron at Gatow and surrounded by lights on poles at each defuelling point for night operations. The points were so arranged that fourteen tanker aircraft could be defuelled at the same time, using two hoses on each aircraft.

From the defuelling terminal, the fuel was pumped to storage tanks erected above ground level and holding 108,000 gallons (490,968 litres) in total. It was then distributed via tanker lorries, and at a later date fuel was also pumped to Havel Lake at the rate of twenty tons of petrol or thirty tons of diesel per hour via a pipeline that had originally been used as part of PLUTO — Pipeline Under the Ocean — to deliver fuel to the Normandy beach-head in 1944. At Havel, the fuel was loaded on to barges, five of which belonged to a Rotterdam shipping company. The *Catalonia* was permanently moored at Havel wharf and used as a storage vessel for the US forces in Berlin; MVs *Algeria*, *California* and *Sardinia* were used to transport fuel to depots in Berlin until April 1949, when the *Sardinia* was transferred to the task of ferrying fuel arriving at Tegel; and the MV *Polonia* was sent to Charlottenburg in January 1949 to act as a fuel storage vessel for the Berlin power station. A sixth vessel, the Belgian-owned *Grimsel*, was used to ferry fuel from the *Catalonia* to the Wannsee for use by the US occupation forces. The six barges made a total of 91 trips, carrying 38,000 tons.

During the whole of the fuel supply operation, the Shell Aviation Company was in charge of the facilities at Gatow and handled a total of 7,312 tankers, discharging 40,020,090 gallons (181,931,329 litres). Defuelling operations at Tegel were controlled by the Standard Oil Company. The principal problem was that there was little standardization in the fuelling equipment used by the aircraft of individual companies, despite the fact that explicit instructions about what was required had been issued in August 1949. This could lead to perilous situations, especially in the case of the Halton tankers, where a lack of adequate fuel tank venting created a concentration of dangerous fumes in the cockpit. As it also caused a major fire risk in the event of a Halton having to make a belly landing, tanker operations by this type of aircraft were suspended on 29 December 1948 and the matter referred to the ARB in London for a ruling. The upshot was that the ARB refused to issue a C of A to any aircraft whose fuel tank extended below the fuselage, as far as the carriage of petrol was concerned, and from 2 February 1949 the Haltons were used exclusively for the carriage of diesel or kerosene.

Meanwhile, the RAF had been experiencing considerable difficulty in controlling the civilian effort through the medium of company liaison officers. The civil companies had shown great enthusiasm, but in a sense their keenness to fly had made it difficult to keep them within the bounds of the operational pattern. A high intensity of operations over a few days was invariably followed by a slump because many of the aircraft were undergoing inspection and maintenance at the same time. Moreover, as the civil operators tended to do things their own way they naturally preferred to do their flying in the daylight hours, and only operated at night when they could spare the crews or to make up for lost sorties caused by a bad weather period.

This had two bad results. First, the preponderance of daylight operations by the civilians threw the RAF's crew and maintenance schedules out of phase, as they had to fill the gaps at night; and secondly, owing to crew shortage and the absence of a proper crew rostering programme, with reasonable rest periods, the crews were showing definite signs of fatigue by the end of October 1948.

In an effort to remedy this state of affairs, a paper was submitted to the Foreign Office on 12 October recommending the pooling of charter companies into groups operating the same type of equipment, so that the surplus resources of one could be used to offset the deficiencies of others. The suggestion was also made that the number of companies and diverse types should be reduced to a minimum compatible with the tonnage requirements and the availability of suitable aircraft. In the event, it was not possible to adopt the first recommendation because of the additional expense involved and the Treasury's insistence on economy; moreover, the operators were also opposed to the idea. However, as far as BEA were concerned, some advance was made in that the direction of the Airlift, instead of being divided between Northolt and Berlin, was passed entirely into the hands of their Manager (Germany), who immediately sent a member of his staff to the advanced HQ of No 46 Group at Bückeburg. The arrival of this officer, who was responsible for liaison with Air Commodore Merer, went a long way towards improving the co-ordination of the civil effort with the RAF.

With the growth of the civil Airlift, combined with a greater influx of American aircraft, which were now operating from Celle and Fassberg in the British Zone, the Berlin airports began to reach saturation point around the middle of November 1948, in spite of the opening of Tegel, and consequently it became more than ever imperative that the allocation of sorties to civil aircraft should be completely utilized throughout the day and night. No definite plan was ever finally agreed, but since it was necessary for some sort of control to be exercised the AOC 46 Group agreed to the allocation of a separate block of beacon times to the civilians at each base instead of allocating the times to the base as a whole. It was then left to BEA to split the civil allocation between the various companies on the basis of aircraft strength and sortie potential.

The month of December was marred by the first fatal casualty of the civil Airlift. On the 8th, Captain Utting, the senior pilot of Airflight, was knocked down and killed by a lorry on the tarmac at Gatow. At the time of the accident, which took place in the early hours, he was walking back to his Tudor aircraft a short distance ahead of his crew when he was struck. He died shortly afterwards at the 84th General Hospital in Spandau. Despite strenuous efforts by the police, the culprit was never found. The death of this highly competent pilot under such tragic and needless circumstances was a sad blow to the civil Airlift.

On 15 December the flying boat base at Finkenwerde was closed and the Short Hythes withdrawn. These three aircraft, named *Hadfield*, *Haslemere* and *Halstead*, had completed 265 sorties and carried over 1,400 tons before ice on the Havel See brought their operations to an end. Also, their speed had made it increasingly difficult to fit them into the traffic pattern. On the following day, an Avro York of Skyways made the 5,000th landing in Berlin.

December had been a very difficult month for the civil Airlift. The combination of the lack of Rebecca and proper de-icing equipment on a great number of aircraft, bad weather, and the need to return a large percentage of the fleet to the UK for conversion to tankers, produced the lowest tonnage for the civilians since August. Better things were expected in the New Year, with the promise of more aircraft and bigger carrying capacity, but the aircrew position was particularly serious. As an example, the one company with ten aircraft operating had only nine crews available, and the civil Airlift as a whole could muster only 1.3 crews per aircraft. In the case of Airflight, only Air Vice-Marshal Bennett was qualified to operate Tudors at night, and following the death of Captain Utting, his only available night captain, Bennett flew two to three sorties every night, with rare exceptions, for a period of nearly two months, an epic of human endeavour which has few parallels in the history of aviation.

The operating companies were urged to redouble their efforts to put things right. Progress was slow, but by the end of the month there were definite signs of improvement. BSAA, who had sent Air Commodore Fletcher out to Wunstorf towards the end of December to investigate ways of stepping up their efforts, had already turned the corner, and in January 1949 produced the excellent result of 3.65 sorties per aircraft day. Air Vice-Marshal Fraser, of Lancashire Aircraft Corporation, came out to Schleswigland to deal with the problems of his unit on the spot, and Sir Alan Cobham of Flight Refuelling promised to send his managing director to Wunstorf to take personal charge of the company's operations.

Unfortunately, in January 1949 the civil Airlift suffered its second fatal accident. On the evening of the 15th, the German driver of a lorry taking six ground engineers of Lancashire Aircraft Corporation to the dispersal area carelessly drove his vehicle in front of an RAF Hastings taxying around the perimeter track. It was impossible for the pilot to avoid a collision, and three engineers and the German were killed by one of the aircraft's propellers. Another engineer was injured, and the other two escaped by jumping out just before the impact. In addition to this accident, a Tudor and a Halifax were seriously damaged by ground vehicles. It was perhaps inevitable, taking into consideration the congestion on the aprons and the number of lorries which had to be used, that accidents of this kind could not be wholly avoided; nevertheless, a number of needless accidents involving surface transport during the winter months caused considerable concern.

In fact, transport was a major problem throughout the operation. There were barely enough vehicles to meet the needs of the RAF, and the civil airlift requirements placed an additional heavy strain on the limited resources available. This handicap was severely felt by the civilians as they were living in more dispersed accommodation than the RAF, and had further to go between their messes, operations rooms and aircraft dispersals. Moreover, the available

Liberator transport G-AHZR of Scottish Airlines, which carried nearly 1,200 tons of liquid fuel to Berlin.

vehicles were not entirely suited to passenger use in winter, and this added to the discomforts of the crews and ground staff, producing a depressing effect on morale.

In January 1949, civilian traffic from Schleswigland and Fühlsbüttel was re-routed into Tegel. This was a great advantage, as it meant that aircraft from both bases could now use the northern corridor on both the outward and inward journeys. Also, the new operating heights of 1,000 ft (305 m) into Tegel and 1,500 ft (547 m) on the return trip considerably reduced the icing risk. This decision, which was made by the AOC No 46 Group, led to an immediate increase in the number of civilian sorties from both bases.

The turn of the tide for the civil Airlift finally came in February 1949. The daily average of sorties went up to 54, and there was a great improvement in the balance between the day and night effort. Only three per cent more sorties were flown by day than by night. The liquid fuel target for the month was passed, a daily average of nearly 400 tons being achieved in the last week of the month. Because of accommodation problems at Wunstorf, however, BSAA's fifth Tudor tanker had to be held back in the UK until the 14th, and Skyways had to continue to operate with only eight or nine crews for five aircraft. Nevertheless, Wunstorf put up an excellent performance during February; with a mean aircraft strength of 42 per cent of the civil fleet, they flew 816 sorties into Berlin, comprising 52 per cent of the civil effort.

Between 5 and 12 February, the four Bristol Freighters operated by Airwork and Silver City were withdrawn. They had carried some very useful loads to Berlin, and had also proved a great asset in flying out bulky loads which had been manufactured in the city. With the arrival of RAF Hastings aircraft in November, their continued use became unnecessary, except for cargo which could not be hoisted to the level of the Hastings' loading door. To handle such items the Americans now had the Fairchild C-82 Packet in operation.

In the middle of January two Liberator tankers were chartered from Scottish Airlines to fill the gap caused by the delay in the arrival of other tanker aircraft. This had caused the stocks of liquid fuel in Berlin to fall to a dangerously low level, and in order to build them up again it was decided to increase the tanker fleet beyond the total of 31 aircraft which had been ordered towards the end of

1948. The Liberators offered a good payload at a reasonable charter price, so the disadvantages of introducing another aircraft type were considered acceptable. The Liberators arrived at Schleswigland on 19 February.

On 20 February the civil Airlift flew its 7,800th sortie in 200 days of operations, during which time it had carried 44,387 tons. The daily average during the first 100 days was 186 tons, rising to 258 tons in the second period.

In March 1949, Flight Refuelling Ltd moved from Wunstorf to Hamburg, in accordance with a decision taken the previous month. HQ No 46 Group also moved from Bückeburg to Luneburg. As March drew to a close, the feeling grew that not only had the winter been overcome, but also that the complex problems of the civil Airlift had been mastered. For the first time, the civilians had developed the full potential of their aircraft resources. The daily number of sorties flown had increased from 54 to 70, and the utilization of serviceable aircraft had risen to an average of three sorties per day. The biggest improvement was in Airflight's sortie rate; their two Tudors flew 144 sorties in March compared with 92 in February, mainly as a result of the adoption of planned maintenance by this company.

Equally as encouraging were the results achieved by the tanker fleet as a whole, and the new target of 350 tons per day was achieved. For the first time, over 10,000 tons of liquid fuel were delivered to Berlin in one month. However, a heavy price was paid before the end of the month, with the loss of six lives in two accidents. The first — which was also the first fatal civil aircraft accident on Airlift operations — occurred on the night of 15 March, when Skyways Avro York G-AHFI (Captain Golding) stalled on the final approach to Gatow and spun into the ground. Six days later, on the return flight from Tegel, Halton tanker G-AJZZ (Captain Freight), belonging to Lancashire Aircraft Corporation, struck some high ground near Schleswigland airfield during a BABS letdown. The sole survivor of the four-man crew was Radio Officer Hamilton, who was thrown 40 ft (12 m) over a hedge and, although seriously injured, managed to walk nearly two miles back to the airfield and report the position

Lancastrian tanker G-AKDS flew over 1,300 hours on the Airlift, carrying 2,784 tons of fuel.

of the accident. After a prolonged stay in hospital, Hamilton returned to flying duties on the Airlift.

Discussions on the long-term plans for the 'wet lift' continued at the end of March, and as the Foreign Office had not yet received confirmation from Berlin that the supply of kerosene from abroad was assured, they initially ordered the conversion of eight Tudor Mk IV aircraft to tankers so that no delay would occur when a decision was finally made. On 1 April, they took a further bold step and authorized the fitting of tanks to four Tudor Mk I aircraft and two Tudor Mk IIs, making a total of fourteen. These would provide an additional reinforcement to the seven already in Germany. Six more Tudor Mk IVs were earmarked for the Airlift, but a decision on the use of these aircraft was postponed. Eight more Lancastrians, in addition to the twelve already operating, could be made available.

Following a meeting in Berlin on 12 April, it was recommended that these arrangements should be amended. It was calculated that the existing tanker fleet could lift a daily average of 450 tons, and that the target of 550 tons, which had now been definitely set for 1 July, could be reached with the addition of the eight Lancastrians. The meeting recommended that the twenty Tudors should have their floors strengthened for dry lift, and that five of them should also be fitted with removable tanks so that they could be operated as tankers in an emergency. As events turned out none of these measures was needed, but it would have been a different story had the blockade continued through a second winter.

Meanwhile, back in Germany, operations were going smoothly. With enough crews to make full use of serviceable aircraft, the civil fleet was now working with the precision of a highly-geared machine. The adoption of planned maintenance by Airflight had encouraged the other operators at Wunstorf to follow their lead, and the result was a marked overall improvement at this base. The Skyways unit had been reinforced by two more Lancastrian tankers, making a total of four. The pressure-fed underground fuelling installation at Wunstorf finally became operational on 19 April, making it possible to tank up a Tudor in about twenty minutes or less, the fuel being delivered at 100 gallons (455 litres) per minute.

In generally favourable weather conditions during April — except for three days when strong crosswinds interrupted operations — a daily average of 73.7 sorties was flown, compared to 70 for March. An outstanding performance was put up by Eagle's Halton freighter, which flew over three sorties per day for the whole month, and this small but efficient company averaged 4.38 sorties per serviceable aircraft day. Sadly, the month's record was once again blemished by a fatal accident. Halton freighter G-AKAC of World Air Freight crashed nine miles (14 km) west of Oranienburg in the Soviet Zone on 30 April on a return night flight from Tegel. Captain Lewis and his three crew lost their lives. This aircraft had maintained an average of two sorties per day to Berlin for 120 days. The accident brought the casualty list of the civil Airlift up to 21 dead. Three fatal crashes had occurred on actual Airlift operations; in addition, another

Avro Lancastrian of Flight Refuelling Ltd in Bermuda after flight-refuelling a Lancastrian III of British South American Airways on the Atlantic run, 1946. Flight Refuelling's expertise was to be vital to the success of the Berlin Airlift.

accident had taken place on 23 November 1948, when a Lancastrian tanker of Flight Refuelling (*G-AHJW*) hit a hill near Thruxton, in England, on a return flight to its home base of Tarrant Rushton for a routine overhaul. As this aircraft was also carrying aircrew passengers, returning to England on leave, the death toll was heavy, eight men — including three aircraft captains — losing their lives.

Six more accidents occurred to civil aircraft in May, fortunately without the loss of any aircrew lives. On the 10th, Lancastrian *G-AKDP* force-landed at dawn, seven miles west of Ludwigslust in the Russian Zone; Captain Tucker carried out a skilful landing, and although the aircraft was written off, the crew were only slightly injured. After treatment in a Russian hospital they were allowed to return to the British Zone and an RAF salvage party recovered the wreckage of their aircraft.

Despite these incidents, which produced an inevitable loss of flying hours, a steady and consistent performance was shown by all the civil operators during May 1949. An outstanding showing was put up by BSAA, which flew 420 sorties against a previous best of 304; the Lancashire Aircraft Corporation, with 464 against 323; and Skyways, with 500 compared to 346. The 3,104 sorties flown was 900 more than the previous highest figure, and for the first time produced a daily average of over 100. The 22,800 tons lifted in the month included a total of 17,988 tons of liquid fuel, the wet lift alone producing a daily delivery of 578 tons. Since the July 1 target had been set at 550 tons, and that with the influx of reinforcement aircraft, the May tonnage was no mean achievement.

There is little doubt that the talks which took place during May 1949 in New

York between the US Secretary of State and the Soviet Envoy spurred the operating companies to greater efforts, their goal now being to take advantage of excellent flying weather to earn as much revenue as possible while the blockade lasted. The performance of Airflight's Tudor G-AGRY is worthy of special mention here; this aircraft flew 115 sorties in thirty days, averaging 3.8 flights per day. This was the best individual performance recorded for any aircraft on the Airlift.

At the end of May Airflight withdrew their two Tudors, as the Foreign Office were now offering reduced rates for charter work and the company would not accept them. It was rather a sorry end to what had been an outstanding performance by anybody's standards. Airflight replaced the Tudors with a Lincoln, on a fortnight's trial, and this aircraft arrived at Wunstorf on 24 June. After conversion to a tanker it flew its first sortie on the 30th carrying 2,500 gallons (11,365 litres).

One major cause for concern during May was the state of the runway at Tegel, which had been built of brick rubble overlaid with a layer of tarmac and had taken a severe hammering. The continuous landings had created undulations in the surface, which affected British aircraft with conventional type undercarriages more than the American C-54s, with their tricycle gear. Work was progressing with all speed on a second runway, scheduled to be brought into use in August; in the meantime, the uneven surface invariably caused aircraft to bounce on landing, and in crosswind conditions the undulations often made a swing develop. This led to a great deal of trouble, particularly with the Haltons, and as the area bordering the runway was soft sand there were a number of incidents involving the collapse of undercarriages. During eight months of operations at Tegel, no fewer than six Haltons were written off as a result of undercarriage failures, and five more were severely damaged.

In May, a number of complaints were received from the Soviet authorities alleging breaches of the flying regulations by civilian aircraft flying as low as 100 ft (30 m) over their airfield at Perleberg. Every one of the complaints was carefully investigated, and proved to be unfounded.

On 11 May the Soviet blockade of Berlin was lifted. At this point, the civil contribution to the success of the Airlift was 86,252 tons, delivered in just over ten months. Although all plans for future expansion of the civil fleet were shelved, civil operations were to continue at the same intensity for a further two months. In the 24-hour period ending at midday on 22 May, the tonnage carried by the civil airlift passed the 1,000 mark for the first time, 1,010 tons being lifted in 133 sorties. The second milestone was reached on 31 May, when Lancastrian tanker G-AKDR (Captain D. Hanbury, DSO) of Flight Refuelling Ltd landed at Gatow at 16:10 local time carrying the 100,000th ton of cargo flown to Berlin by civil aircraft. To mark the occasion, the AOC-in-C, Air Marshal T.M. Williams, flew in the aircraft, a gesture that was much appreciated by the civilians. It was particularly fitting that this particular crew had been chosen to undertake this flight, for it was Captain Hanbury who had flown the very first civil cargo to Berlin in this same aircraft.

The final phase of the civil lift took place between 1 June and 15 August 1949. For the sixth month in succession, June saw the civilians break all records, despite a reduction of six aircraft in the fleet strength and the fact that although weather conditions were reasonable, it was not a particularly good month for the time of year. The tonnage exceeded May's figure by 380 tons, while the 3,205 sorties flown beat the previous best by 101. On the wet lift, the loss of an estimated 1,275 tons of liquid fuel caused by the withdrawal of Airflight was offset mainly by the improved performance of the Schleswigland group of Halton tankers. The daily average of 586 tons was the highest wet lift figure ever recorded, and was the culminating effort of the tanker fleet. Flight Refuelling Ltd recorded a particular success, flying a record number of 825 sorties. This was due in no small measure to the efforts of Mr H. Johnson, Flight Refuelling's Senior Executive (Flying), who had been sent out to Germany by Sir Alan Cobham in February and who had subsequently reorganized and revitalized his unit.

June's intensive effort resulted in a bad crop of accidents, bringing about the loss of 102 aircraft days — double the figure for May. Halton tanker G-AKBJ of Lancashire Aircraft Corporation was written off in a landing accident at Tegel on 1 June; Halton freighter G-AITC of World Air Freight was seriously damaged in a landing accident at Fühlsbüttel on 10 June, the aircraft being unserviceable for the remainder of the month; Halton tanker G-ALBZ of Lancashire Aircraft Corporation was written off in a landing accident at Tegel on 12 June, the crew escaping with slight injuries except for the radio officer, who spent nearly a month in hospital; Skyways York G-ALBX was written off on 19 June following a crash-landing in a field shortly after take-off from Wunstorf; Skyways Lancastrian tanker G-AKFH was written off in a landing

The crew were lucky to escape unhurt when Lancastrian tanker G-AKFH crashed and burned at Gatow.

accident at Gatow on 26 June and the aircraft completely destroyed by fire, the crew getting away with superficial burns; and there were other, less serious accidents involving two Haltons, two Lancastrians and a Liberator.

On 13 July the contracts for Lancashire Aircraft Corporation, British American Air Services, Scottish Airlines and Westminster Airways were cancelled, and civil operations at Schleswigland came to an end. Similarly, the four Lancastrian tankers of Skyways, operating from Wunstorf, were withdrawn on 17 July, four days after the Lincoln tanker of Airflight. The liquid fuel target had now been reduced to 140 tons daily, and this figure remained in force until 15 August, when the wet lift finally ended. During this period, BSAA were retained to lift 100 tons and Flight Refuelling Ltd forty tons daily, a task which both companies accomplished with ease.

In the meantime, the remaining ten freighters had continued at full intensity throughout July, producing a record dry lift of 5,945 tons despite extensive periods of fog and low stratus.

The decision to end the civil Airlift was finally taken at the end of July, and on 15 August the last civil sortie on Operation 'Plainfare' was flown by Halton G-AIAP (Captain Villa) of Eagle Aviation. This aircraft, carrying 14,400 lb (6,532 kg) of flour, landed at Tegel at 01:45 hours local time on 16 August, and so brought to an end the greatest transport operation in the history of civil aviation. Its success had been due entirely to the skill, devotion and resourcefulness of the air and ground personnel of no fewer than 23 British charter companies, together with BOAC and BSAA. A total of 103 aircraft had been involved at different periods, although the numbers engaged at any one time had varied between 31 and 47. In just over a year, these aircraft had flown 21,921 successful sorties to Berlin, carrying a load of 146,980 tons. This figure was almost double the total tonnage of mail and freight carried by all British civil aircraft on scheduled services in the 23 years from 1924 to 1947.

Lancastrian tanker G-AKFF carried one of the biggest fuel tonnages to Berlin, uplifting 3,022 tons in 449 sorties.

Chapter Seven
Airlift humour

Airlift humour inevitably poked fun at adversity and made light of the very real dangers to which the crews were subjected. An RAF York pilot, Flight Lieutenant 'Frosty' Winterbottom, was one of the most prolific humorists; his wit came in the form of various sketches that adorned the walls of the Malcolm Club Aircrew Canteen at Wunstorf, and their value in boosting morale was immeasurable. One portrayed the terrified crew of a York approaching Gatow and in the process of receiving a message from the GCA controller. It said: 'Hello York 274. Understand you are lost in cloud on three engines, icing up, hydraulics jammed and short of fuel. Visibility here is 800 yards. Cloud base 200 feet. Repeat after me: "Our Father which art in heaven ...".'

One morning, after publication of a newspaper article to which the RAF crews took exception, Winterbottom portrayed a York in the circuit at Wunstorf flying through intense ground defence anti-aircraft fire. On the ground, the Adjutant was airily explaining to the startled Station Commander that a rumour had gone round to the effect that the Press Correspondent concerned was aboard the aircraft.

The Russians suffered similar shafts of frosty wit. One Winterbottom sketch showed their fighter pilots at a Met briefing. A gloomy official forecast surface haze, icing and 10/10ths coal dust at 5,000 ft (1,524 m) in the corridor. 'Hardly the weather for Yak flying, comrades,' he concluded. Russian aircraft, incidentally, were invariably known as 'Joe's Boys'. It was not unusual for Russian fighters to formate on aircraft in the corridor in conditions of poor visibility, and often the first indication a pilot had of Russian fighters in his vicinity was the Approach Controller's 'You are not alone,' uttered in sepulchral tones.

The ground crews' perennial war with the aircrew was often carried into the pages of the Form 700. On one notable occasion, a vague pilot scrawled 'Something loose in Compartment G'. The response from a sardonic rigger was, predictably, 'Something tightened in Compartment G'.

Many of the amusing incidents that brightened the months of intense activity arose from the fact that the Americans and British were serving together. The peculiarities of syntax and accent were a never-ending source of misunderstanding, both accidental and deliberate. At Gatow, the main flow of humour was between the British controllers and American pilots; the British pilots, with the exception of those flying the civilian Tudors, tended to be businesslike and earnest rather than jocular. Sadly, the extent to which Airlift humour depended on physical factors of speech make it difficult, if not impossible, to transpose most of the best jokes into prose. For example, an American pilot with a rich, deep and drawling Alabama accent ('dis heah's Air Fo'ce Two Fohty Foh'), coming into Gatow, was asked by a British controller in a tone of genuine enquiry: 'I say, old boy, are you from Boston?' Without the voices this is only mildly funny, yet at the time there was loud laughter from Gatow to Danneberg, fifty miles (80 km) down the corridor.

The Americans were startled by the appearance of the Bristol Wayfarer and Freighter, with their fixed undercarriages. The story is told of an American Skymaster pilot who requested the identity of one of these aircraft ahead of him on the approach. Gatow Control informed him that it was a Wayfarer, and the American, deliberately misunderstanding, retorted in astonished tones: 'The MAYFLOWER? You guys sure are throwin' in everything!'

They nicknamed another civil aircraft 'Hoppity-hoppity'. Great were the rejoicings on the R/T as 'Hoppity' kangarooed its way down the runway, its progress punctuated by comments such as 'Say, Hoppity, you wanna bounce left at the end, boy!' The pilots in a line of Skymasters waiting to take off would invariably criticize landing techniques, and it was woe betide the pilot who bounced. His arrival would be accompanied by a chorus in unison of 'ONE! ... TWO! ... THREE! ... FOUR! ... ' and so on down the runway. To add to his embarrassment, Gatow Control would chip in with a comment like 'When you've finished with our runway, would you *please* put it back?'

One of the civil Tudors once tore through the overshoot area, its tailwheel sending up clouds of dirt and dust. A plaintive voice from Gatow Control asked: 'Don't you *care* what happens at the other end?'

Returning to the fun provided by accents, a British controller on Approach Control at Gatow called a C-54 and was answered in the most exaggerated Oxford accent. The controller was not deceived. Imitating an American accent, which he could do very well, he called back: 'Which of you guys got a goddam Limey aboard?'

Catchwords and phrases were concocted to suit certain recurrent incidents. For instance, an aircraft taxying with its flaps down would soon be told 'Hey, 123, don't look now, but your slip is showing'. Then there was the 'Who Dat' menace, a relic from the war days. A voice, usually deep South, would say out of the blue, 'Who dat down dere?' whereupon Control was in honour bound to reply 'Who dat up dere sayin' who dat down dere?' — and so it would go on, with further complications from aircraft ahead and behind saying 'Who dat up front sayin' who dat down dere saying' who dat up here sayin' who dat down dere?' It all seems terribly childish in retrospect, but it helped to relieve the stress and the boredom of the Airlift.

Aircraft landing at Gatow had to pass over the Kaiser Wilhelm Tower and the Havel See. The names given to the Tower were many and varied, including the Christmas Tree (an allusion to the lighting), Bill's Bones and the Monarch's

Mausoleum. The Havel was variously called the River, the Ditch and the Pond, but the favourite expression was 'passing water'.

The employment of WRAF R/T operators intrigued the Americans, and it was not unusual for a voice to whisper over the R/T — a quite useless precaution — 'Hey, bud, is Betty there?' The controller would at once become hard of hearing, and coax the caller along until he was shouting his amorous intentions to the world.

The numbers of the Skymasters were used as callsigns, but the pilots and controllers soon substituted nicknames for the prosaic numerals. 200 became 'Two double nothin', 'Two tons' or 'Double-C', while 222 was 'Triple Deuce'. 225 was variously 'Two and a quarter', 'Two bits' and 'Two quarters', while 244 was always 'Fohty-foh' from the southern accents of her pilots. 237, for no known reason was 'Shorty George', 211 was 'Snake-eyes' and 212 'Boxcars', both derived from craps-shooting. Predictably, 333 and 555 — both RAF types — were always called 'State Express'.

The Tudor pilots of British South American Airways were in perpetual high spirits, and answered to the generic name of 'Charles'. The enormous aircraft came under verbal fire from the Americans on many occasions, such as the time when a C-54 pilot was told by the tower to stand by until the next aircraft had landed. 'Do you mean that thing in the sky over there?' he asked. 'She's not a thing,' said the incoming Tudor pilot, 'she's a very nice little aeroplane.' As the Tudor touched down, the American commented, in a tone of great wonder, 'Jeez — it is an airplane, too'.

The presence of Canadian aircrew, flying with the RAF, caused a few misunderstandings. On one occasion, hearing a transatlantic voice coming from an aircraft which, according to the book, should have been an RAF Dakota, a controller asked: '123, are you a Skymaster?' The transatlantic voice replied, 'Ah don't think so. Ah'll take a look. Ah wuz a Dakota when Ah took off, but maybe Ah've growed some.'

The reporting of cargoes caused some amusement. RAF pilots always mentioned what they were carrying when they made their initial contact with Berlin. There was the pilot who reported his load as 'a mixed load of coal, flour dried fruit and two Brigadiers'; and then there was the man with ten thousand bottles of gin, who had to put up with a stream of exhortation to 'land her gently' all the way from the Frohnau Beacon to Gatow.

One rather erudite jest, notable more for its spontaneity than for anything else, was made by a York pilot. He was on the runway, about to take off, and an aircraft was on the approach. Control called him in some agitation: 'York X, clear to roll as quickly as possible'. The pilot, as his aircraft moved forward, replied in academic tones: 'This is York X — like Yser, rolling rapidly'. The snap quotation from the poem 'Hohenlinden' had not gone unnoticed by another British pilot, who had been asked to stack over the Frohnau Beacon. 'Steady on, old man, I've only got an Elementary School Certificate!'

It was the Americans who started the legendary rhyming jingles on the air when reporting their load over the Frohnau Beacon. A Skymaster pilot broke the ice one day with the most famous couple of all: 'Here comes a Yankee with a blackened soul, Headin' for Gatow with a load of coal!'

More than 11,000 aircraft were landed at Gatow by GCA, and the controllers were not unnaturally the butt of a good deal of humour. A popular sketch showed a smoking four-engined aircraft in a crumpled state after making a belly landing on the airfield. At the door of the GCA caravan, the startled controller was confronted by an irate and slightly damaged crew, demanding in laboured tones: 'WILL YOU KINDLY REPEAT YOUR LAST TRANSMIS-SION?!!' Yet another portrayed a GCA controller transmitting to an aircraft: 'Coming in very nicely, track good, glide path excellent, maintain 275 degree … very nice … very nice indeed … ' In the murky background, a large four-engined aircraft could be seen approaching to land, about 100 ft (30 m) above the runway — and upside down.

The following true story came from Fassberg. An American PFC (Private) was informed that his wife was sick in hospital and under observation for acute stomach trouble. That was not all, as became clear when a Red Cross official gently read the remainder of the report. 'Your baby is also in hospital with severe tonsilitis,' he continued. 'The other four children are at home under the care of the Red Cross and neighbours. Two of them have measles; the other two have mumps.' There followed a long and thoughtful pause. Then the PFC asked: 'How's mah dawg?'

The Germans contributed to the general humour, too, but usually without realizing it. Among the passengers brought out of Berlin one dark and dirty night was a gnarled crone of some eighty years, who was hoisted, uncomplaining, into the back of a York freighter and dumped among the mailbags. At 04:00 hours she landed at Wunstorf (cloud base 300 ft (91 m) visibility half a mile (805 m)) and was lowered safely to the ground, apparently quite unmoved by the black and bumpy trip. Then the trouble started. She took one look at the three-ton truck which was to take her to Hannover and refused to board it. It looked too dangerous!

During Group Captain Biggar's time as OC RAF Station Fassberg, American C-54 Skymasters began operating from the base on a large scale. Down in the loading area, buildings sprang up almost overnight. Visiting a newly-constructed cookhouse on the flight line one morning, the Group Captain was hailed by a typically boisterous US Top Sergeant, who asked how he should address the RAF officer. 'Well, I'm the Group Captain', Biggar replied. 'OK, Cap'n,' said the American cheerfully, and 'Cap'n' it was forever after. On this particular occasion the Sergeant had water and equipment troubles. The Group Captain agreed to lay on a daily water-bowser run, and to make structural alterations to improve cooking facilities. Such ready co-operation almost over-whelmed the Sergeant, who determined to reciprocate to the best of his ability.

'Say, Cap'n,' he said confidentially, 'any time you feel like a nice steak and eggs, just you come down to my cookhouse. And say,' he continued, throwing a quick glance over his shoulder at the Group Captain's WRAF driver, 'I can fix you up with a couple of pounds of coffee for your popsie, any time you say!'

Chapter Eight
The final months

The early weeks of 1949 marked one of the most tense periods of the Airlift. In January and February the tonnage of supplies flown into Berlin surpassed all previous records, and the Russians — perhaps for the first time — realized that they had involved themselves in a dilemma from which there was no graceful retreat. They had not believed it possible for the Western Allies to mount an operation of this magnitude, let alone sustain it in all kinds of weather, but once it was in full swing there was nothing they could do about it short of shooting down the Allied transport aircraft, which — since the Allies had legal access to Berlin via the three air corridors — would have constituted an act of war.

They could, however, do a lot to harass the Airlift without resorting to force, and this appeared to be their policy during the early weeks of 1949, when British and US Intelligence sources indicated that additional Soviet Air Force fighter and bomber units were arriving on airfields in the Russian Zone. Shortly afterwards, the Russians began what seemed to be a large-scale air exercise; Allied transport crews flying along the corridors reported that the Russians appeared to be constructing air-to-ground firing ranges directly below their flight paths.

Admittedly, the sight of Soviet aircraft in and around the corridors, conducting firing practices, was nothing new. On 1 October 1948, at least ten American pilots had reported Russian fighters engaged in firing practices, and on that same day the British authorities lodged a strong protest when two Yaks buzzed a Bristol Wayfarer of Silver City Airways. The pilot, Captain Michael Davidson, stated that one Yak broke off its mock attack only fifty yards or less (46 m) from the nose of his aircraft, adding drily: 'As a former RAF pilot, I would describe the Russian attack approach as awful!' Despite such protests, the British and American crews began to encounter increasing numbers of Soviet aircraft in the corridors early in 1949, and incidents multiplied. The Soviet types involved were mainly Il-10s, Yak-3s and La-9s, and the tactics employed by their pilots were varied and often ingenious.

One of the Soviet pilots' favourite tactics was to fly at high speed along the corridors, either singly or in formation, and usually in the opposite direction to the transport traffic stream, and then make a fast head-on pass at a transport, pulling up sharply at the last minute. In the ten months from August 1948 to May 1949, American transport crews alone reported 77 buzzing incidents by

Soviet aircraft in the corridors, together with another 96 incidents that were loosely described as close flying. The Americans also stated that Russian fighters fired cannon and machine-guns in the vicinity of transport aircraft on 14 separate occasions, although no instance of a deliberate attack was recorded.

What the Russians called 'routine air-to-ground firing practices' were frightening enough, though seldom dangerous. The Soviet fighters would orbit over the corridors in the vicinity of one of their firing ranges, flying singly or in pairs at about 6,000 ft (1,829 m), above the main stream of traffic. They would then go into a shallow dive towards the range, passing immediately in front of the transport aircraft with their guns firing all the way down. American pilots recorded 42 such incidents, and on 54 occasions they also reported Soviet anti-aircraft fire in the corridors, although the gunners were careful to place their shells well clear of the transport aircraft.

Searchlights were the most common nuisance; the corridors were lined with batteries of them and they made accurate night flying — which was absolutely essential in such a high traffic density – very tiring. USAF C-54 pilots reported 103 occasions when the Russians exposed searchlights, apparently with the intention of causing harassment. Other Soviet incidents reported by US crews during the Airlift period included close flying (96 incidents), flares (590), ground-to-ground fire (55), explosions observed on the ground (39), chemical laying (54) and bombing (36). The Russians also tried jamming the Allied radio frequencies, both by the use of primitive countermeasures equipment and by the simpler expedient of ordering their pilots to use the frequencies as much as possible, filling the already overcrowded ether with Russian chatter. There were 82 reported incidents of this kind.

Some incidents brought the Allied air forces in Europe, including the UK-based squadrons, to full alert. On 24 January 1949, for example, when a Dakota of RAF Transport Command crashed in the Russian Zone near Lübeck, it was not known for some time whether the aircraft had been deliberately shot down, and whether this was the start of a general offensive by the Russians against the aircraft using the corridors, and in the meantime the Allied air forces stood ready for action. There was a similar alert when a second RAF Dakota came down in Russian territory in March.

If it had come to a shooting war in the early part of 1949 there is no doubt that the Allied tactical air forces in Europe could have given an excellent account of themselves. General LeMay's fighter groups were now almost fully equipped with F-80 Shooting Stars, while the fighter squadrons of the British Air Forces of Occupation (formerly 2nd Tactical Air Force) were rapidly re-equipping with Vampire jet fighter-bombers. The Lincoln heavy bomber squadrons of RAF Bomber Command, together with SAC's British-based B-29 groups, could also have delivered a formidable weight of explosives on strategic targets in eastern Europe.

The RAF Dakota crash of 24 January was, in fact, a tragic accident out of which the Russians made a lot of capital, as German civilians were involved. At 16:30 that day, *KP491* was one of four Dakotas which touched down at Gatow

Wing Commander Frank Carey, wartime fighter ace and renowned fighter leader, pictured in the cockpit of his Tempest II. Carey was leader of the Gutersloh Wing during the early months of the Airlift.

in quick succession to disgorge its cargo of coal. As soon as the sacks were unloaded, women cleaners set to work with brooms, sweeping the fuselage clean of any spillage which, in turn, was gathered up from the tarmac. There was not, nor could there afford to be, any wastage. The whole operation took fifteen minutes, and at 16:45 KP491 began taking on board its new cargo: 22 passengers who were being evacuated from Berlin for various reasons. At exactly 17:00, Pilot II E.J. Eddy lifted the Dakota from Gatow's runway and set course in the darkness, following the headings passed to him by Navigator II L. Senior. The third member of the crew was Signaller II E. Grout.

The flight to Lübeck was scheduled to take an hour and a half, and for the first few minutes it was pleasant enough. Most of the passengers had never flown before, and the sight of the Russian Zone's lights twinkling beneath them was a thrilling experience. Gradually, however, the ground was lost to sight as the aircraft began to run through cloud, and many of the passengers drifted off to sleep. They awoke to severe turbulence as the Dakota flew through dense cloud. Some of them vomited and the children, who were seated at the front with the women passengers, started to cry. Signaller II Grout left his position for a while and went back to make sure that the passengers' seat belts were properly fastened and tight; it was an action that, in minutes, was undoubtedly to save a number of lives.

At 18:20 Eddy began a gradual descent through cloud towards Lübeck, lowering the undercarriage and following GCA instructions that would bring him down to his break-off height of 300 ft (91 m). The turbulence was still severe, and the pilot had to fight hard to control the Dakota as it lurched its way down the glidepath. Suddenly, there was a jolt accompanied by a series of loud bangs on the fuselage floor, followed immediately by a sound of tearing metal. Moments later, the Dakota crashed into a forest and burst into flames. The aircraft came to rest wedged at an angle between two massive tree trunks, its

Eine Dakota weniger – eine Lehre mehr

Die Flugzeugkatastrophe
von Schönberg

Die Unfallstelle

'One Dakota less — one Lesson more' reads
the caption to this photograph in the Russian-
controlled Berliner Illustrierte, *showing the*
wreck of KN491.

nose about fifteen feet (4.6 m) off the ground and the tail a little lower down.
The front of the aircraft was now completely alight and the fuselage was filling
with smoke as two of the male German passengers wrestled with the main
hatch. Eventually they managed to open it partially. Jumping out, they ran
around to the nose of the aircraft, only to be forced back by the heat of the
flames.

By this time other passengers were also making their escape, albeit with great
difficulty, for a tree trunk was jammed against part of the main door. The two
Germans, whose names were Zeidler and Brandis, helped to pull two of them to
safety through a window. They also discovered the pilot, lying unconscious
near the aircraft's nose among some debris; one of his legs was injured and he
was bleeding badly. People were still trapped in the blazing wreck, but there was
nothing anyone outside could do; the heat and the flames were too intense.
Besides, Zeidler and Brandis were the only two who had escaped without injury.

As soon as they had made sure that everyone was safely clear of the Dakota,
in case of an explosion, Zeidler and Brandis set out to get help, stumbling
through the woods in pitch darkness. After a while they found a path which
took them out of the trees and to the edge of a marsh; beyond it they could see
lights, stretching across the horizon, and felt certain that this was Lübeck
airfield. They set out across the marsh, sinking up to their ankles in mud and
slimy undergrowth. Then they encountered a fresh obstacle: a deep, fast-
flowing stream. They were wondering how to get across it when they saw a
solitary light, some distance away on the right. It turned out to be a farmhouse,

and the farmer willingly offered to take them to the nearest police station. It was only when they were entering the building that they realized they were still in the Russian Zone.

It was now 20:45. As soon as Zeidler and Brandis had told their story the police acted quickly, assembling bandages and medical supplies. Accompanied by Zeidler, a patrol set off for the wreck and gave first aid to the passengers, some of whom were now in a serious condition, until a lorry-load of Russian soldiers arrived. The casualties were taken to a nearby village, where emergency treatment was given by a German doctor and an innkeeper provided food and blankets. An ambulance came and took the more seriously injured to hospital in Schöneberg, and shortly afterwards the dead were taken there too: five German civilians and the RAF wireless operator, Signaller II Grout. The survivors who remained in the village were subjected to a thorough interrogation by the Russians throughout the early hours of the following morning, then they too were taken to the hospital, where they were given a breakfast of white bread, scrambled eggs and butter. Zeidler, who thought it was the best meal he had eaten for a long time, asked one of the hospital staff if it was part of the normal diet in the Russian Zone. He was told that it was very special indeed; the Russians worked on the basis that people in hospital were of no use to the state and were therefore not worth feeding.

All the morning papers in the Soviet Zone carried the story of the crash. One of them — *Vorwärts* — carried as its main headline the words: *Airbridge – Deathbridge*, with the sub-heading *Senseless Evacuation of Berlin Children Causes Tragic Victims*. The story ran: 'A British Dakota carrying 22 passengers, including seventeen children, and a crew of three, left Gatow Airport yesterday and crashed near the Anglo-Russian zonal border near Schöneberg late last night.

'Search parties, led by Russian officers and personnel were sent out immediately, according to information given by British officials. It is thought the crash occurred in a wood.

'The crash of the aircraft carrying children near the zonal border has created an atmosphere of tension among parents who have registered their children to fly out of Berlin.

'Early in the morning the first calls were received by West Sector offices to remove children's names from the registration lists. Anxious mothers said it would not be necessary to send their children to the Western Zone if the Western Powers could reach agreement. More and more parents are realizing that they need not live in continual anxiety about the journey of their children if they had registered in the East Sector for their food and coal rather than remaining in the Western Sectors.'

'*One Dakota Less — One Lesson More*', trumpeted the Russian-controlled *Berlin Illustrierte* a few days later, in an article that carried photographs of the wrecked and burnt-out Dakota, bodies at the scene of the crash and survivors in hospital. The caption under one photograph, which depicted the tail section of the aircraft with the serial number clearly visible, read:

'The survivors tell of three terrible shocks just as they were about to land.

"Everything was thrown about in the aircraft, we tried to escape by the windows and half-open door, the unconscious were burned to death ... " They were victims of the Western political sabotage against the East Zone which caused the blockade of Berlin. All would still be alive if the Western powers had not used Berlin as a centre for the "cold war".'

The final death toll of the crash of *KP491* was eight — seven passengers and Signaller II Grout. Zeidler and eight other passengers — including a child — who were not seriously injured were released in the early hours of 27 January and permitted to cross the Zone border into the city of Lübeck; the remainder, including the RAF pilot and navigator, followed later when they had recovered from their injuries sufficiently to travel.

The Royal Air Force was to suffer two more fatal crashes before the end of the Airlift. The second one of 1949, which happened on the night of 22 March, also occurred in bad weather when Dakota *KJ970* was approaching to land at Lübeck. The crew consisted of Flight Lieutenant M.J. Quinn of the Royal Australian Air Force, Flying Officer K.A. Reeves as navigator and Master Signaller A. Penny. Quinn and Reeves were killed outright, and Penny died later of his injuries.

The last crash involving an RAF aircraft occurred during the run-down of Operation 'Plainfare' in the summer of 1949. In the early morning of 16 July, Hastings *TG611* suffered engine failure shortly after taking off from Tegel and plunged into the ground, killing all five crew. They were Flying Officer I.R. Donaldson (pilot), Sergeant J. Toal of the Glider Pilot Regiment (co-pilot), Navigator I W.G. Page, Signaller II A. Dunsire, and Engineer II R.R. Gibbs.

Early in January 1949, a directive was issued by HQ BAFO that Operation 'Plainfare' was to be regarded as a long-term commitment, and that future planning should be undertaken on the assumption that it was likely to continue for another two or three years. The assumption was based on the fact that talks on the Berlin issue were getting nowhere, and that the Russians were showing signs of strengthening their military presence in the Eastern Zone. From No 46 Group's viewpoint, the main implications of the directive were fourfold. First of all was the urgent necessity to relieve the aircrews, most of whom had been flying continuously on the Airlift since July 1948; associated with this problem was the need for Transport Command to recommence some measure of training on the strategic air routes and a limited amount of transport support training with the Army.

The second requirement was the introduction of some alternative system governing the rotation of ground personnel. Until now, ground staff had been sent back to the UK after a three-month tour in Germany, but experience had shown that the continuous turnover of personnel on the Airlift stations tended to reduce the latter's operational efficiency and caused a good many administrative problems. There was also the question of 2,400 RAF National Servicemen — cooks, drivers, mechanical transport personnel, equipment assistants, radar fitters, wireless operators and general duties clerks — who had been due for release in September 1948, but who had been retained for an indefinite period;

trained replacements would have to be found for them from somewhere before long. Thirdly, domestic accommodation at the Airlift airfields would have to be greatly improved to bring them up to the standard required for long-term operations; and fourthly, improvements were needed to the operational facilities on the airfields, in particular the provision of a third runway at Gatow.

On 16 February 1949, a conference was held at the Air Ministry to discuss the long-term development of Operation 'Plainfare' and to make appropriate recommendations. Among these, and probably the most important, was one that individual RAF transport squadrons engaged on the Airlift should alternate a tour of three months in Germany with two months in the United Kingdom, where they would undertake continuation, support and route training and so obtain a much-needed rest from Airlift operations. The rotation would be staggered, and in effect three-fifths of the total Transport Command squadrons would be engaged in 'Plainfare' at any one time.

Another recommendation was that the target for the average daily airlift for the RAF should be 1,000 short tons (2,000,000 lb/907,200 kg). This would involve the creation of a potential lift of 1,400 short tons (2,800,000 lb/ 1,270,080 kg) per day to compensate for periods of bad weather. In fact, this RAF target was almost the same as the minimum target set to the RAF and Civil Airlift in September 1948, although during the critical winter months this combined target had been the maximum possible tonnage that could be uplifted.

The USAF had been quicker off the mark in establishing a rotation procedure for Operation 'Vittles' personnel. Towards the end of September 1948, a Replacement Training Unit had been established under the direction of MATS at Great Falls, Montana, to train C-54 aircrew, and in December sufficient replacement crews were coming through this pipeline to permit the replacement of temporary duty personnel. When it became apparent that the number of incoming personnel arriving in Germany for Great Falls would be adequate to permit the rotation of TDY personnel, and at the same time provide a steady gain in personnel assigned to the Airlift, it was decided that all crew members could be rotated back to the United States after a six-month tour. By February 1949 this rotational policy was firmly established and rotation of crew personnel to the USA was occurring regularly and without hitches.

January 1949 also saw changes in the system by which RAF aircraft were despatched to Berlin. Earlier in the Airlift, a continuous despatch system had been possible because RAF aircraft were equipped with Eureka and distance-measuring equipment and also carried navigators. This meant that they were able to arrive at a given point at a given time within acceptable limits of accuracy. USAF C-54s, on the other hand, did not carry navigators; all navigation was done by the pilot, relying mainly on radio compasses. This meant that USAF pilots had to depend on dead reckoning based on forecast winds, the accuracy of which was variable.

In order to ensure the most even flow of traffic the USAF had introduced a four-hour block system of despatches; each of the two bases in the American

Zone was allotted alternate four-hour periods in which to despatch its aircraft, the interval between aircraft being determined by the forecast weather conditions at the Berlin terminal coupled with the rate at which GCA could cope with the arriving aircraft. The first obvious drawback to this system was that it created lengthy periods of standby time caused by numerous aircraft lining up prior to their scheduled take-off time in order to fill each available space in the block. During the period when the four-hour block system was in force, it was not unusual to see twenty to thirty aircraft lined up near the take-off position with their engines idling. To overcome this, the block times were eventually reduced to a one-hour cycle, each base being allocated time in proportion to its number of aircraft.

When USAF C-54s began to operate from Fassberg, and many different types of civil aircraft joined the Airlift, the RAF no longer found it possible to operate a continuous despatch system. The obvious answer was to adopt the American four-hour block system, but this produced immediate problems in that for the best utilization of available resources, aircraft had to complete the round trip to Berlin and be ready for the next block within a four-hour period or risk a long wait. Although four hours was the optimum time for a C-54 to complete a cycle, the Yorks and Dakotas needed rather longer for two main reasons: they had longer distances to fly (Celle and Fassberg were nearer to the northern and central corridors than the bases used by the RAF) and, as they carried a higher proportion of non-standard loads than the American aircraft, they took longer to load and unload.

However, it was not until January 1949 that the penalties being paid by the RAF through using the four-hour block system became obvious enough for action to be taken. As a result, a two-hour block system was introduced, and this went some way towards ironing out the peak loads and improving aircraft utilization by ensuring that an aircraft too late for one block did not have to wait up to four hours for the next. By the end of April 1949 Fassberg, Celle and Wunstorf were operating an hourly despatch system, with each airfield in succession flying off a wave of aircraft at three-minute intervals, the whole despatch lasting an hour.

So complex was the problem of air traffic control that the one-hour system, which for a time was thought to be as near ideal as the prevailing conditions allowed, was found to have an unforseen disadvantage. With the reduction in the time period of each block, the number of aircraft in the block was naturally less; Wunstorf, for example, had previously despatched twelve aircraft in a period of 33 minutes, but under the one-hour system it despatched eight aircraft in 21 minutes in the first hour and four aircraft in nine minutes in the second hour. The disadvantage was that under the old system there was plenty of time for the crew of any of the first seven or eight aircraft to transfer to a standby if their own aircraft became unserviceable and still get away within the time block. In a wave of eight aircraft only the first two or three crews could make the transfer, and in a wave of four there was no time for any transfer at all.

At any one time in the early weeks of 1949, the RAF and the civil charter companies had a maximum of 138 aircraft assigned to Operation 'Plainfare', split up as follows. Wunstorf — 36 Yorks, five Lancastrians and four Tudors; Fühlsbüttel — nine Haltons and seven Lancastrians; Lübeck — forty Dakotas; Schleswigland — 26 Hastings and 11 Haltons. The USAF's Operation 'Vittles' had 225 C-54s assigned to it, although the actual figure of aircraft operationally engaged was 192 on average. During February 1949, these 192 aircraft were in the air 25 per cent of the time; during 39 per cent of the time they were undergoing maintenance, while 36 per cent of the time was spent on the ground loading, unloading, refuelling or because of bad weather. At all times, there was an average of 48 US aircraft in the air in all three corridors.

By February 1949 the Airlift was running almost like clockwork, with an average daily uplift of some 5,500 short tons (11,000,000 lb/4,989,600 kg) — 1,000 tons above the December average. Nevertheless, there was a certain element of luck behind this achievement. Had the weather been as severe as it normally was, the supplies available in Berlin would almost certainly have fallen below the minimum winter requirements laid down by the Allied military governors. By good fortune, the average temperatures for the three worst winter months — December to February — were much the same as those to be expected in an average late autumn or early spring. One weather hazard, however, which did affect the tonnages landed in Berlin was fog; in November 1948 this had caused the daily average to fall to 3,800 tons by dislocating the flying schedules, all Airlift aircraft having been grounded for one or two days.

On 15 March 1949 HQ No 46 Group moved from Bückeburg to Luneburg. The main reason behind the move was that office accommodation at Bückeburg, following the expansion of the Group headquarters in December 1948, proved completely inadequate. Moreover, telephone communications between Bückeburg and the Airlift bases were poor and were physically incapable of improvement. Also, Luneburg was geographically more centrally located in relation to the Airlift stations in the British Zone.

On 1 April, HQ No 46 Group was placed under the command of the AOC-in-C BAFO for all purposes, and on 1 May the personnel were posted from the Transport Command to the BAFO establishment. The effect of the squadron rotation scheme and the complete transfer of No 46 Group to the BAFO establishment was that HQ BAFO was now entirely responsible, both operationally and administratively for British Airlift operations in Germany. The aircraft, which belonged to Transport Command, returned periodically to the United Kingdom as before for base servicing, but the aircrews were attached to BAFO during their three-month tour in Germany.

Also on 1 April, the Civil Airlift Division (British European Airways) was formed, and the officials of the corporation responsible for the administrative supervision of the civil charter companies engaged on the Airlift were embodied in it. Those who, at the same time, had been involved in other duties would now be free to concentrate entirely on the problems of the Airlift. To ensure the closest possible co-ordination of RAF and civil charter operations, the Civil Airlift Division joined HQ 46 Group at Luneburg on 1 May.

Meanwhile, the Airlift bases had witnessed a steady flow of VIP visitors. Among them was the British Prime Minister, Clement Attlee, who arrived at Gatow on 3 March, accompanied by Lord Henderson (Parliamentary Under-Secretary for Foreign Affairs) at the start of a three-day visit to inspect the British Airlift operation. The VIPs were met at Gatow by General Sir Brian Robertson, the British Military Governor, Major-General Bourne, OC British forces in Berlin, and Professor Ernst Reuter, the Mayor of West Berlin. Attlee was visibly impressed by what he saw, describing the Airlift as 'one of the wonders of the world'. It was exactly the kind of morale-boosting exercise the hard-worked Airlift personnel needed.

Another big boost for morale occurred on 16 April, when — in a 24-hour period ending at noon on that day — the Combined Airlift Task Force, in the course of 1,398 flights, lifted 12,940 tons of food, coal and machinery into Berlin. This tonnage, the equivalent of 22 trains each of fifty freight cars, handsomely beat the previous daily record of 8,246 tons set up on 11 April. Of the total, 10,904 tons were delivered by the Americans and 2,036 tons by the British. The achievement was described by one RAF spokesman as 'unparalleled in the history of air transport,' while General Clay, the US Military Governor, declared that at the rate set up on 15-16 April 'we will be able to bring in more food to Berlin by air than we brought in by rail and road before the blockade.'

It was a somewhat optimistic statement, but its significance was not lost on the Russians. Neither was something else. On 4 April, 1949, the North Atlantic Treaty was signed in Washington by twelve nations — Belgium, Canada, Denmark, France, Iceland, Italy, Luxembourg, the Netherlands, Norway, Portugal, the United Kingdom and the United States. Article 5 of the Treaty was quite specific: an armed attack against one or more of the member nations in Europe or North America would be considered an attack against them all. This was further elaborated in Article 6: ' ... An armed attack on one or more of the Parties is deemed to include an armed attack ... on the forces, vessels, or aircraft of any of the Parties, when in or over these territories (ie territories under the jurisdiction of any of the parties in the North Atlantic area north of the Tropic of Cancer) or any area of Europe in which occupation forces of any of the Parties were stationed on the date when the Treaty entered into force ...'

The North Atlantic Treaty was the final nail in the Soviet Union's 'divide and conquer' policy in Europe. Moreover, the last sentence of Article 6 left the Russians in no doubt over one matter. If they attempted at this stage to use force against the visible success of the Airlift, the Western Allies would go to war collectively against them.

The Russians were now in a dubious, not to say absurd, position. Their blockade of Berlin had failed lamentably, and their leaders knew it. There had been changes in Moscow, too; the Soviet Defence Ministry received a considerable shake-up, with Marshal Nikolai Bulganin replaced as Defence Minister by his deputy, Marshal Alexander Vassilievsky, who was in turn replaced by Marshal Sokolovsky, recalled from Germany. Sokolovsky was replaced as Military Governor of the Soviet Zone by General Vassily Chuikov, veteran of Stalingrad and a very able commander, to whom the German garrison in Berlin had surrendered in 1945.

The Russians were thus faced with the problem of extricating themselves from the Berlin situation without too much loss of prestige, and it was events in China which gave them a much-needed pretext. In January 1949, following a series of reversals for his Nationalist armies at the hands of Mao Tse-Tung's Communist forces, Generalissimo Chiang Kai-shek had resigned the presidency of China. The Communists had completed their occupation of Manchuria, captured Peking and were pushing southwards towards Nanking, their opponents disintegrating almost everywhere. It was only a matter of time before the whole of China was absorbed into the Communist structure. The Kremlin had failed in its bid to dominate Europe, but to bring China into the net was a coup of massive proportions. Under these conditions the stranglehold on Berlin, albeit reluctantly, could be loosened.

In the closing days of April, reports began to reach the Western Allies that the Russians were about to lift the blockade. In fact, discussions to this end had been going on in the United Nations for some weeks, and they culminated in a Soviet offer to lift the blockade if a date could be set for a meeting of the Foreign Ministers of the four powers to discuss the long-standing currency question. Earlier, the Russians had made the postponement of constitutional plans for West Germany a precondition for ending the siege, but now they no longer insisted on this; in any event, the Western powers had already stated that nothing would deflect them from their intention to set up a West German government, and they would not agree to a meeting of Foreign Ministers while the blockade lasted.

On 4 May, the four powers at last reached an agreement. All restrictions imposed on traffic to and from Berlin by all parties were to be removed on 12 May 1949, and a meeting of the Foreign Ministers was to take place in Paris on 23 May. On 8 May the Parliamentary Council in Bonn adopted a constitution for the new Federal Republic of Germany. It was four years to the day since Germany's unconditional surrender. Twenty-four hours later, General Chuikov issued the order lifting all traffic restrictions with effect from one minute past midnight on 12 May.

He was as good as his word. At 00:01 hours on 12 May 1949, the lights came on once more in the Western Secors of Berlin. At the same time, the first Allied convoys crossed the border into the Soviet Zone, and the railway line was reopened with the departure of a British military train bound for Berlin. It was hauled by a Soviet Zone locomotive handled by a West German crew.

The twelfth of May was a holiday in Berlin. Factories, shops and schools were closed for the day, and crowds flocked into the streets to cheer the arrival of the first convoys. There were tearful reunions as relatives who had been stranded in western Germany for ten months came home.

At Schöneberg, the City Assembly held a special meeting to mark the occasion, and also to bid farewell to General Clay, who was retiring from office

Left *Police wait to accompany a food convoy destined for Berlin.*

Right *Convoys of supply trucks, Berlin-bound, await the signal that the blockade has ended at a checkpoint on the border.*

Far right *The first truck-load of food to arrive in Berlin at the end of the blockade is greeted with wreaths of flowers.*

as US Military Governor after four years. His popularity was undoubted; as he entered the council chamber, the whole assembly rose spontaneously to give him a standing ovation. Then the members paid silent tribute to the 54 British and American airmen who, at that time, had lost their lives on the Airlift. It was unanimously decided to rename the square outside Tempelhof Airport 'Air Bridge Square' in their memory.

The relief and the sense of euphoria were not to last. Within a matter of hours, the Russians began to impose fresh restrictions on traffic movements; among other things, they insisted that all rolling stock travelling to and from Berlin should be pulled only by Soviet Zone locomotives, and they needlessly delayed the issue of navigation permits for barge traffic. West German commercial vehicles were debarred from using the autobahn on the pretext that this was reserved for Allied military traffic.

Then came a new and more serious complication. At midnight on 20 May, 15,000 West Berlin railwaymen employed by the Soviet-controlled Reichsbahn came out on strike to enforce a claim for payment of their wages in Westmarks, the reinstatement of dismissed workers, and recognition of their union, the independent UGO. Within a few days, the railway system throughout the Soviet Zone came to a standstill. In the days that followed, bloody battles were fought between the strikers and police; the violence ceased when armed West Berlin police took over all railway stations and drove out strikebreakers who had been brought in by the Communists. The strike, however, continued, and the railway — the primary link between the Western Zones and Berlin — remained paralysed.

Once again, it was the Airlift that came to the rescue. The decision was taken to continue both 'Plainfare' and 'Vittles' at their existing intensity until the rail, road and canal traffic were fully restored and a reserve of supplies had been built up in the city as an insurance against a future breakdown of surface communications. It is interesting to note that the daily average British lift of 1,920 short tons (3,840,000 lb/1,741,824 kg) throughout June was its highest

in any month during Operation 'Plainfare', and that on several days during the month the tonnage exceeded 2,000.

The Airlift continued to operate at a reduced rate until 1 August 1949, on which date it was decided that a gradual rundown should begin, culminating in the withdrawal of all aircraft by 1 October. On the first day of August the C-54s of the 317th Troop Carrier Wing ceased operating from RAF Station Celle, and were withdrawn a few days later; the contracts for the civilian fleet expired on 10 and 15 August and were not renewed, so the aircraft returned to their respective bases in the United Kingdom; on 15 August the number of Dakotas at Lübeck was reduced to 32, while No 206 Squadron with its twelve Yorks and 47 Squadron with its nine Hastings returned to Lyneham and Topcliffe respectively, the former to disband in February and re-form later as a maritime reconnaissance unit.

On 22 August the ten Yorks of No 59 Squadron returned to Bassingbourn. They were followed, on the 29th, by No 18 Squadron, whose ten Dakotas flew back to Waterbeach. This unit also disbanded in February 1950, to re-form in 1953 within RAF Bomber Command with Canberras at Scampton. The ten Yorks of No 511 Squadron also returned to Lyneham on 29 August; the squadron converted to Hastings in September and flew these on Transport Command routes throughout the world until it was renumbered No 36 Squadron on 1 September 1958. On 15 December 1959 No 511 was re-formed as the second RAF squadron with Bristol Britannias, which it used until its disbandment in January 1976.

By 1 September, all Dominion personnel who had been engaged in Airlift duties had been returned to the United Kingdom. Also on this day, the Combined Airlift Task Force was disbanded and the C-54s of the 60th Troop Carrier Wing ceased operations from Fassberg, all aircraft and personnel being withdrawn during the month. Nos 30 and 10 Squadrons, each with ten Dakotas, flew back to Abingdon and Oakington on 12 and 26 September respectively.

Currency reforms led to the reappearance of goods in the shops of the Western Zones.

On 10 October, the Hastings force at Schleswigland was reduced to sixteen aircraft — representing the total number of RAF transport aircraft now remaining in BAFO. Five days later, HQ No 46 Group was closed down at Luneburg and returned to the United Kingdom. It was intended that the two squadrons of Hastings at Schleswigland should be transferred to Fassberg and remain there as a nucleus in case it proved necessary to reopen the Airlift at a later date, but this policy was later changed and the aircraft were diverted to Wunstorf, RAF Fassberg being placed under the command of HQ No 85 Group and reduced to care and maintenance basis on 1 November 1949.

Historian Paul R. Wood, a staff member of the RAF Air Historical Branch, summed up the broad achievement of the Airlift in an assessment which appeared in the *Royal Air Force Quarterly* in the autumn of 1958.

'In all, 2,325,809 short tons were flown into Berlin between late June 1948 and early September 1949, the tonnage delivered after 12 May 1949 (when the blockade was lifted) being a measure of the West's determination not to be caught again without an adequate stockpile. Of this total, a surprising 1,586,530 tons were coal, while food accounted for 538,016 tons and the wet fuel lift by British civil aircraft 92,282 tons. In percentage terms, the United States Air Force contributed 76.7 per cent, the RAF 17.0 per cent and British civil aircraft 6.3 per cent.

'From the RAF point of view feelings of satisfaction were not untinged with disappointment. Nearly 400,000 tons had been lifted into Berlin by RAF aircraft, flying in all weathers and under conditions requiring a high level of professional competence, with a daily average of over 1,100 tons sustained in May, June and July 1949. The most strenuous efforts had been made by air and ground crews alike for months at a time, and yet for all this the average daily totals had fallen to 710 tons between October 1948 and February 1949 — a fact predicted in Air Staff assessments.

'The reasons for this trough are complex. Winter weather would inevitably take its toll and very obviously the time block system introduced into the British Zone with the arrival there of American aircraft had a most damaging effect. Other handicaps were the two special tasks carried out by the RAF: the lifting of awkward freight, which delayed the loading and unloading of aircraft, and the carriage back to the British Zone of passengers (mostly children, old people and the sick) and freight (particularly goods manufactured in Berlin for sale in the West). In all, 34,240 tons of freight were carried in this way.

'The RAF suffered too from the shortcomings of the aircraft which it had to operate during what was basically an interim period in the development of its transport fleet. The Dakota still maintained a reasonable level of serviceability, but being a smaller carrier compared with the C-54 or the York it was the first to lose its place in the time block system when weather or some other factor disrupted the flow; serviceable aircraft were therefore left standing idle. The York, nearly comparable to the C-54 in terms of load, suffered from bad bouts of unserviceability, due mainly to the fact that, being developed from the Lancaster bomber, it lacked the high degree of sturdiness required for frequent take-offs and landings with full loads, although as a long range transport it gave good service. The Hastings, too, introduced in November 1948, had its teething problems and, with its conventional type of undercarriage, had difficulty with crosswinds and was not allowed to take off or land when the crosswind component was calculated at more than twenty knots; while the C-54 with its tricycle undercarriage was able to operate in considerably more severe conditions. A number of Hastings sorties were lost to the RAF in the course of the Airlift for this reason.

'More important, perhaps, was the fact that the utilization rate for RAF transport aircraft — agreed after long debate and in response to repeated calls for economies in defence expenditure — was low compared with that obtaining in the American transport force. The latter had on average twice as many crews available per aircraft as the RAF, and maintenance backing to match, the British preferring a larger force whose utilization rate could be increased (it was hoped) in case of emergency to a smaller force operating at full stretch. In the event, it was possible by drawing on the resources of other Commands to make maintenance provision for a substantial increase in York flying hours; the aircrew problem, however, was less tractable: with no final decision by the summer of 1948 on the size of the peacetime air force, decisions on career structure were inevitably deferred, with effects on both recruitment and the retention of existing personnel. Nor was it possible to transfer other RAF aircrew to transport duties without a period of training and without jeopardising the efficiency of other Commands.

'With a shortage of aircrew and the problems with the time block system increasing as the C-54 force grew in numbers, it seemed likely that the tonnage delivered by the RAF would stabilize at around 1,000 tons a day once the Hastings was in full operation — a figure below the transport force's potential in terms of aircraft and maintenance backing. The April average was only a fraction short of this figure, and deliveries for the remaining months of the Airlift were comfortably above it.

'The RAF's task therefore was to make the most of a situation not of its own choosing. It had demonstrated at the beginning of the Airlift how rapidly it could respond to an emergency: the Dakota and York force had been operating from Wunstorf within 24 hours of the order being given and the tonnage which it delivered in July and August while the C-54s were deploying was vital in sustaining the Allied position. The first Hastings squadron too had been deployed to Germany well ahead of schedule. More significant, the emphasis which the previous Commander-in-Chief of Transport Command, Sir Ralph Cochrane, had put on training and accident prevention, had been more than justified by the high standards of flying under the exacting conditions of the Airlift, and by the fact that there were only five serious accidents to RAF aircraft, although costing a total of seventeen RAF personnel killed.

'In the end it was transport aircraft which won a notable victory and the RAF transport force which helped to sustain Britain's position in the alliance, 23 per cent of the total tonnage delivered being perhaps no mean contribution in the conditions of the time. The irony of the situation, however, comes in the postscript. Success in the Airlift could not save Transport Command from further cuts, it being perhaps inevitable in the circumstances of 1949 that what money there was to spend would be devoted to other Commands. A resurgence of the transport force would have to await events beyond the confines of Europe.'

As far as the USAF's Military Air Transport Service was concerned, its participation in Operation 'Vittles' was, in a sense, a dress rehearsal for another emergency which, when the Berlin Airlift ended, was ony a year away. June 1950 saw the start of the 'hot' war in Korea, and to MATS fell the responsibility of airlifting supplies across the Pacific to the United Nations forces. The C-47 took the biggest share of in-theatre transport operations, but it was the C-54 — augmented by the newer Boeing C-97s and, after 1952, the Douglas C-124 Globemasters — which bore the brunt of the transpacific work.

During the Korean War, MATS delivered 80,000 tons of cargo and 214,000 troops to Korea. Compared to the tonnages delivered to Berlin, it was a drop in the ocean, but the operation taught the USAF a number of valuable lessons.

Ready for home: air and ground crews of US Navy Squadron VR-6 at Rhein-Main celebrate the end of the blockade.

The Airlift memorial stands in the Platz der Luftbrücke — Airbridge Square — near Tempelhof.

One of them was that the MATS airlift force must be an active force, ready to go anywhere in the world right at the start of a crisis, and the second one was that larger transports were preferable and more cost-effective than a fleet of smaller ones. The originator of that doctrine, and the man in charge of the Korean air supply operation, was General William H. Tunner, former commander of the Combined Airlift Task Force that had won the first and bloodless round of the Cold War in Berlin.

Yet that battle would have been lost without the staunch and unfailing optimism and support of the Berliners themselves. If there is to be a last word, let it be spoken by Lieutenant Gail Halversen, the young American who endeared himself to countless Berlin children and their families.

'... No sooner had the propellers stopped turning than our engineer opened the door and there were three or four Berliners standing right in that door. The truck was ready to back up by the time we stopped and was already backing by the time our props stopped turning. They looked at those sacks of flour and you could tell what they meant to them. I think that this was their ticket to freedom, that if enough of those sacks came through they'd be able to stay in Berlin, they'd be able to stay free, and they looked at us Americans as we came down between the sacks with respect and a smile on their faces, put their hands out, and gave us a slap on the back; and yet *they* were the heroes.'

Appendix One
Monthly tonnages

Month	US		British		Total	
	Flights	*Tonnages*	*Flights*	*Tonnages*	*Flights*	*Tonnages*
26 June – 31 July 1948	8,117	41,188	5,919	29,053	14,036	70,241
August	9,796	73,632	8,252	45,002	18,048	118,634
September	12,905	101,871	6,682	36,556	19,587	138,427
October	12,139	115,793	5,943	31,245	18,082	147,038
November	9,046	87,963	4,305	24,629	13,351	112,592
December	11,655	114,572	4,834	26,884	16,489	141,456
January	14,089	139,223	5,396	32,739	19,485	171,962
February	12,051	120,404	5,043	31,846	17,094	152,250
March	15,530	154,480	6,627	41,686	22,157	196,166
April	19,129	189,972	6,896	45,405	26,025	235,377
May	19,365	192,247	8,352	58,547	27,717	250,794
June	18,451	182,722	8,049	57,602	26,545	240,324

Civil Airlift: Individual aircraft performances

Aircraft		Freighter			Tanker			Total		
Type	Reg'n	Sorties	Hours	Tonnage	Sorties	Hours	Tonnage	Sorties	Hours	Tonnage
Air Contractors Dakota	G-AIWC	172	466.44	613.5	–	–	–	172	466.44	613.5
	G-AIWD	53	154.35	192.4	–	–	–	53	154.35	192.4
	G-AIWE	161	445.30	570.7	–	–	–	161	445.30	570.7
		386	1,066.49	1,376.6	–	–	–	386	1,066.49	1,376.6
Airflight Tudor	G-AGRY	85	299.24	749.1	421	1,165.51	3,658.7	506	1,395.15	4,407.8
	G-AKBY	–	–	–	415	1,156.14	3,575.8	415	1,156.14	3,575.8
Lincoln	G-ALPF	1	2.49	7.1	45	115.11	425.9	46	118.00	433.0
		86	232.13	756.2	881	2,437.16	7,660.4	967	2,669.29	8,416.6
Airwork Bristol Freighter	G-AHJD	58	174.32	290.6	–	–	–	58	174.32	290.6
	G-AICS	16	44.12	80.0	–	–	–	16	44.12	80.0
		74	218.44	370.6	–	–	–	74	218.44	370.6
Air Transport(Cl) Dakota	G-AJVZ	205	562.10	742.6	–	–	–	205	562.10	742.6
Aquila Airways Hythe	G-AGER	6	19.45	32.6	–	–	–	6	19.45	32.6
	G-AGIA	118	322.34	632.3	–	–	–	118	322.34	632.3
	G-AHEO	141	358.19	744.3	–	–	–	141	358.19	744.3
		265	700.38	1,409.2	–	–	–	265	700.38	1,409.2
British American Air Services Halton	G-AIAR*	–	–	–	247	789.16	1,805.5	247	789.16	1,805.5
	G-AKBB	48	119.13	237.1	25	86.42	149.8	73	205.55	386.9
	G-AKGN	49	114.03	287.7	292	876.44	1,982.8	341	990.47	2,270.5
		97	233.16	524.8	564	1,752.42	3,938.1	661	1,985,58	4,462.9
British Nederland Air Services Dakota	G-AJZX	76	230.03	276.4	–	–	–	76	230.03	276.4
British South American Airways Tudor	G-AGBZ	–	–	–	517	1,423.12	4,391.9	517	1,423.12	4,391.9
	G-AGRH	114	322.13	1,134.2	–	–	–	114	322.13	1,134.2
	G-AGRJ	117	319.22	1,178.2	–	–	–	117	319.22	1,178.2
	G-AKCA	–	–	–	529	1,432.32	4,480.9	529	1,432.32	4,480.9
	G-AKCB	–	–	–	454	1,229.23	3,832.4	454	1,229.23	3,832.4
	G-AKCC	–	–	–	446	1,211.29	3,818.8	446	1,211.29	3,818.8
	G-AKCD	–	–	–	385	1,035.12	3,288.8	385	1,035.12	3,288.8
		231	641.35	2,312.4	2,331	6,331.48	19,812.8	2,562	6,973.23	22,125.2
British Overseas Airways Corporation Dakota	G-AGIZ	21	58.11	76.2	–	–	–	21	58.11	76.2
	G-AGNG	33	89.38	119.8	–	–	–	33	89.38	119.8
	G-AGNK	27	76.21	98.0	–	–	–	27	76.21	98.0
		81	224.10	294.0	–	–	–	81	224.10	294.0

Aircraft		Freighter			Tanker			Total		
Type	Reg'n	Sorties	Hours	Tonnage	Sorties	Hours	Tonnage	Sorties	Hours	Tonnage
Bond Air Services										
Halton	G-AHDN	139	391.55	757.2	–	–	–	139	391.55	757.2
	G-AHDO	295	670.27	2,089.2	–	–	–	295	670.27	2,089.2
	G-AHDP	243	591.03	1,354.4	–	–	–	243	591.03	1,354.4
	G-AHDS	436	997.14	2,833.1	–	–	–	436	997.14	2,833.1
	G-AHDT	70	291.26	384.8	–	–	–	70	291.26	384.8
	G-AHDU	363	854.28	2,505.1	–	–	–	363	854.28	2,505.1
	G-AHDW	65	235.44	357.5	–	–	–	65	235.44	357.5
	G-AHDX	180	621.16	1,092.3	–	–	–	180	621.16	1,092.3
	G-AIOI	129	305.32	877.7	–	–	–	129	305.32	877.7
	G-AIWN	292	646.08	2,189.4	–	–	–	292	646.08	2,189.4
	G-ALON	204	458.08	1,489.3	–	–	–	204	458.08	1,489.3
	G-ALOS	161	362.27	1,201.4	–	–	–	161	362.27	1,201.4
		2,577	6,425.48	17,131.4	–	–	–	2,577	6,425.48	17,131.4
Ciros Aviation										
Dakota	G-AIJD	91	268.48	330.9	–	–	–	91	268.48	330.9
	G-AKJN	237	661.39	846.5	–	–	–	237	661.39	846.5
		328	930.27	1,177.4	–	–	–	328	930.27	1,177.4
Eagle Aviation										
Halton	G-AIAP	390	885.23	2,727.8	–	–	–	390	885.23	2,727.8
	G-AIAR†	60	132.25	432.0	–	–	–	60	132.25	432.0
	G-ALEF	227	545.27	1,481.4	–	–	–	227	545.27	1,481.4
	G-AJBL	377	907.47	2,662.6	–	–	–	377	907.47	2,662.6
		1,054	2,471.02	7,303.8	–	–	–	1,054	2,471.02	7,303.8
Flight Refuelling										
Lancastrian	G-AGWI	–	–	–	226	579.14	1,381.0	226	579.14	1,381.0
	G-AGWL	–	–	–	361	881.25	2,422.6	361	881.25	2,422.6
	G-AHJU	–	–	–	438	1,175.59	2,429.1	438	1,175.59	2,429.1
	G-AHJW	–	–	–	40	130.20	221.0	40	130.20	221.0
	G-AHVN	–	–	–	279	657.28	1,586.1	279	657.28	1,586.1
	G-AKDO	–	–	–	431	1,141.02	2,683.0	431	1,141.02	2,683.0
	G-AKDP	–	–	–	378	1,053.53	2,216.9	378	1,053.53	2,216.9
	G-AKDR	–	–	–	526	1,472.04	3,070.1	526	1,472.04	3,070.1
	G-AKDS	–	–	–	480	1,305.31	2,784.5	480	1,305.31	2,784.5
	G-AKFF	–	–	–	449	1,129.14	3,022.5	449	1,129.14	3,022.5
	G-AKFG	–	–	–	439	1,099.38	2,943.0	439	1,099.38	2,943.0
	G-AKTB	–	–	–	391	985.33	2,354.8	391	985.33	2,354.8
		–	–	–	4,438	11,611.21	27,114.6	4,438	11,611.21	27,114.6
Hornton Airways										
Dakota	G-AKLL	108	301.25	397.5	–	–	–	108	301.25	397.5
Kearsley Airways										
Dakota	G-AKAR	84	234.35	301.6	–	–	–	84	234.35	301.6
	G-AKDT	162	445.22	587.0	–	–	–	162	445.22	587.0
		246	679.57	888.6	–	–	–	246	679.57	888.6
Lancashire Aircraft Corporation										
Halton	G-AHCX	–	–	–	151	481.52	873.4	151	481.52	873.4
	G-AHWN	78	237.41	492.4	230	793.03	1,345.3	308	976.44	1,837.7
	G-AHYH	–	–	–	313	1,007.20	1,827.5	313	1,007.20	1,827.5
	G-AIHV	–	–	–	282	886.29	1,640.6	282	886.29	1,640.6
	G-AIHY	26	63.35	178.6	180	585.04	1,285.5	206	648.39	1,464.1
	G-AILO	–	–	–	98	312.20	583.9	98	312.20	583.9
	G-AJZY	–	–	–	228	733.04	1,282.7	228	733.04	1,282.7
	G-AJZZ	–	–	–	89	273.45	493.5	89	273.45	493.5
	G-AKBJ	–	–	–	195	645.38	1,138.7	195	645.38	1,138.7
	G-AKBK	–	–	–	289	905.10	1,709.5	289	905.10	1,709.5
	G-AKEC	79	220.57	544.3	80	257.11	488.6	159	478.08	1,032.9
	G-AKXT	–	–	–	242	733.03	1,358.0	242	733.03	1,358.0
	G-ALBZ	–	–	–	200	633.41	1,170.7	200	633.41	1,170.7
		183	522.13	1,215.3	2,577	8,193.40	15,197.9	2,760	8,715.53	16,413.2
Scottish Airlines										
Dakota	G-AGWS	51	126.29	175.9	–	–	–	51	126.29	175.9
	G-AGZF	50	127.45	172.2	–	–	–	50	127.45	172.2
Liberator	G-AHDY	–	–	–	233	733.52	1,534.0	233	733.52	1,534.0
	G-AHZP	15	36.42	110.1	–	–	–	15	36.42	110.1
	G-AHZR	–	–	–	148	489.21	1,182.5	148	489.21	1,182.5
		116	290.56	458.2	381	1,223.13	2,716.5	497	1,514.09	3,174.7

Aircraft		Freighter			Tanker			Total		
Type	Reg'n	Sorties	Hours	Tonnage	Sorties	Hours	Tonnage	Sorties	Hours	Tonnage
Silver City Airways										
Bristol Freighter	G-AGVB	65	199.21	292.3	–	–	–	65	199.21	292.3
	G-AGVC	73	210.00	324.4	–	–	–	73	210.00	324.4
Bristol Wayfarer	G-AHJC	38	105.23	141.7	–	–	–	38	105.23	141.7
	G-AHJO	37	105.07	138.0	–	–	–	37	105.07	138.0
		213	619.51	896.4	–	–	–	213	619.51	896.4
Sivewright Airways										
Dakota	G-AKAY	32	87.06	116.1	–	–	–	32	87.06	116.1
Skyflight										
Halton	G-AIWP	16	44.21	106.7	–	–	–	16	44.21	106.7
	G-AKBR	24	61.22	169.4	–	–	–	24	61.22	169.4
		40	105.43	276.1	–	–	–	40	105.43	276.1
Skyways										
York	G-ALBX	467	1,279.16	4,616.6	–	–	–	467	1,279.16	4,616.6
	G-AHFI	147	411.29	1,364.3	–	–	–	147	411.29	1,364.3
	G-AHLV	467	1,259.43	4,194.2	13	38.44	108.8	480	1,298.27	4,303.0
Lancastrian	G-AKBT	–	–	–	459	1,229.02	3,437.6	459	1,229.02	3,437.6
	G-AKFH	–	–	–	196	507.55	1,675.9	196	507.55	1,675.9
	G-AKMW	–	–	–	479	1,265.17	3,600.7	479	1,265.17	3,600.7
	G-AKSN	–	–	–	228	590.45	1,950.2	228	590.45	1,950.2
	G-AKSO	–	–	–	293	766.05	2,540.0	293	766.05	2,540.0
		1,081	2,950.28	10,175.1	1,668	4,397.48	13,313.2	2,749	7,348.16	23,488.3
Transworld Charter										
Viking	G-AHON	37	101.47	130.3	–	–	–	37	101.47	130.3
	G-AHOT	81	220.59	285.1	–	–	–	81	220.59	285.1
		118	322.46	415.4	–	–	–	118	322.46	415.4
Tent Valley Aviation										
Dakota	G-AJPF	186	504.25	665.5	–	–	–	186	504.25	665.5
World Air Freight										
Halton	G-AKAC	255	602.26	1,776.4	–	–	–	255	602.26	1,776.4
	G-AKGZ	7	16.25	45.0	–	–	–	7	16.25	45.0
	G-AKTC	264	593.45	1,881.8	–	–	–	264	593.45	1,881.8
		526	1,212.36	3,703.2	–	–	–	526	1,212.36	3,703.2
Westminster Airways										
Dakota	G-AJAY	44	127.10	159.7	–	–	–	44	127.10	159.7
	G-AJAZ	184	527.55	664.3	–	–	–	184	527.55	664.3
Halton	G-AHDL	–	–	–	10	33.45	64.4	10	33.45	64.4
	G-AHDM	176	450.35	928.0	106	351.25	815.7	282	802.00	1,743.7
	G-AHDV	–	–	–	136	455.50	824.5	136	455.50	824.5
	G-AHNW	–	–	–	116	367.48	887.3	116	367.48	887.3
		404	1,105.40	1,752.0	368	1,208.48	2,591.9	772	2,314.28	4,343.9
Grand total (All aircraft)		8,713	22,640.00	54,634.8	13,208	37,156.36	92,345.4	21,921	59,796.37	146,980.2

* This aircraft hired out to Eagle Aviation is a freighter after completion of tanker duties with BAAS.
† This aircraft hired from BAAS.

Operation 'Plainfare': RAF units employed in support, June 1948–September 1949

Headquarters, CALTF
Headquarters, No 46 Group
RAF Station Wunstorf
RAF Station Gatow
RAF Station Lübeck
RAF Station Schleswigland
RAF Station Fassberg
RAF Station Celle
Air Traffic Control Centre (Bad
    Eilsen)
Task Force Approach Control
    (Berlin)

No 10 Squadron (Dakota C IV)
No 18 Squadron (Dakota C IV)
No 24 Squadron (York C 1 and one
    Lancastrian II, *VL980*)
No 27 Squadron (Dakota C IV)
No 30 Squadron (Dakota C IV)
No 40 Squadron (York C 1)
No 46 Squadron (Dakota C IV)
No 47 Squadron (Hastings C 1 —
    the first to equip with the type)
No 51 Squadron (York C 1)

No 53 Squadron (Dakota C IV,
    Hastings C 1 from August 1949)
No 59 Squadron (York C 1)
No 62 Squadron (Dakota C IV)
No 77 Squadron (Dakota C IV)
No 99 Squadron (York C 1)
No 201 Squadron (Sunderland
    GR V)
No 206 Squadron (York C 1)
No 230 Squadron (Sunderland
    GR V)
No 242 Squadron (York C 1)
No 297 Squadron (Hastings C 1)
No 511 Squadron (York C 1,
    Hastings C 1 from September
    1949)
No 240 OCU (Dakota C IV)
No 241 OCU (York C 1)

RAAF Detachment
RNZAF Detachment
SAAF Detachment
Nos 4, 5 and 11 GCA Units

Appendix Four
Operation 'Plainfare': Casualties

Royal Air Force casualties

York MW288 19 September 1948
Crashed at Wunstorf after engine failure following night take-off. All crew killed.

Crew:	175967	Flt Lt H. W. Thomson	–	Pilot
	166759	Flt Lt G. Kell	–	Co-Pilot
	1604758	Nav II L. E. H. Gilbert	–	Navigator
	1577861	Sig II S. M. L. Towersey	–	Signaller
	1881703	Eng II E. W. Watson	–	Flight Engineer

Dakota KP223 17 November 1948
Crashed at night inside the Russian Zone near Lübeck airfield when approaching to land in bad weather. Crew killed immediately except for Flt Lt Wilkins who died of his injuries later.

Crew:	1316810	Pilot I F. I. Trevona	–	Pilot
	55636	Flt Lt J. G. Wilkins	–	Navigator
	3001781	Sig III P. A. Lough	–	Signaller
	2221594	Sgt F. Dowling	–	Passenger

Dakota KN491 24 January 1949
Crashed at night inside the Russian Zone near Lübeck airfield when approaching to land in bad weather. Sgt Grout was killed and the other two members injured. In addition, seven German passengers were killed and a number of others injured.

Crew:	575250	Pilot II E. J. Eddy	–	Pilot
	1594259	Nav II L. Senior	–	Navigator
	1375129	Sig II L. E. Grout	–	Signaller

Dakota KJ970 22 March 1949
Crashed at night inside the Russian Zone near Lübeck airfield when approaching to land in bad weather. Crew killed immediately except for Sgt Penny who died of his injuries later.

Crew:	A412688	Flt Lt M. J. Quinn, RAAF	–	Pilot
	59342	Fg Off K. A. Reeves	–	Navigator
	552860	M Sig A. Penny	–	Signaller

Hastings TG611 16 July 1949
Crashed early morning at Tegel immediately after take-off. All crew killed.

Crew:	59756	Fg Off I. R. Donaldson	–	Pilot
	7597167	Sgt J. Toal, Glider Pilot Regt	–	Co-Pilot
	1324598	Nav I W. G. Page	–	Navigator
	1826137	Sig II A. Dunsire	–	Signaller
	5030958	Eng II R. R. Gibbs	–	Engineer

Civil Airlift casualties

Airflight Limited 8 December 1948

Capt Clement Wilbur Utting

Ground accident at Gatow, Berlin, Germany.

Flight Refuelling Limited 23 November 1948

Capt Cyril Taylor
Capt Reginald Merrick Watson Heath
Capt William Cusack
Nav Off Michael Edwin Casey
Nav Off Alan John Burton
Rad Off Dornford Winston Robertson
Flt Eng Kenneth Arthur Seaborne

Aircraft accident at Thruxton, England.

Lancashire Aircraft Corporation 15 January 1949

Gd Eng Theodor Supernatt
Gd Eng Patrick James Griffin
Gd Eng Edward O'Neil

Ground accident at Schleswig-land, Germany.

Lancashire Aircraft Corporation 21 March 1949

Capt Robert John Freight
Nav Off James Patrick Lewin Sharp
Eng Off Henry Patterson

Aircraft accident at Schleswig-land, Germany.

Skyways Limited 15 March 1949

Capt Cecil Golding
First Off Henry Thomas Newman
Rad Off Peter James Edwards

Aircraft accident at Gatow, Berlin, Germany.

World Air Freight 30 April 1949

Capt William Richard Donald Lewis
Nav Off Edward Ernest Carroll
Eng Off John Anderson
Rad Off Kenneth George Wood

Aircraft accident 20 miles from Tegel, Berlin.

Appendix Five
Operation 'Plainfare': Accidents to RAF aircraft requiring salvage

Date	Aircraft	Aircraft serial	Category	Location
21 Jul 48	Dakota	KN641	AC	Schipol
22 Jul 48	Dakota	KN213	AC	Gatow
26 Jul 48	Dakota	KN252	E2	Near Fassberg
28 Jul 48	York	MW315	AC	Gatow
3 Aug 48	Dakota	KN507	AC	Bückeburg
3 Aug 48	Dakota	KN238	E1	Gatow
3 Aug 48	York	MW199	AC	Wunstorf
17 Sep 48	Dakota	KN631	AC	Lübeck
20 Sep 48	Dakota	KN355	AC	Lübeck
21 Sep 48	York	MW288	E2	Wunstorf
25 Sep 48	York	MW245	E1	Wunstorf
9 Oct 48	Sunderland	SZ528	AC	Finkenwerder
10 Oct 48	York	MW305	E1	Gatow
12 Oct 48	Dakota	KN523	B	Bückeburg
1 Nov 48	Dakota	KN424	B	Lübeck
6 Nov 48	Dakota	KN521	B	Gatow
11 Nov 48	York	MW270	E1	Wunstorf
19 Nov 48	Dakota	KN223	E2	Duffenest (Russian Zone)
22 Nov 48	York	MW234	B	Wunstorf
3 Dec 48	York	MW246	E1	Gatow
14 Dec 48	York	MW300	E1	Gatow
15 Dec 48	York	MW238	B	Gatow
4 Jan 49	Dakota	KN567	AC	Bückeburg
15 Jan 49	York	MW232	B Fly	Gatow
25 Jan 49	York	MW229	AC	Wunstorf
26 Jan 49	Dakota	KN491	E2	Russian Zone
6 Feb 49	Hastings	TG525	B Fly	Tegel
10 Mar 49	Lancaster	PA380	A Assistance	Schleswigland
19 Mar 49	York	MW297	AC	Wunstorf

23 Mar 49	Dakota	KJ970	E2	2 miles from Lübeck
29 Mar 49	York	MW308	AC	Wunstorf
4 Apr 49	Hastings	TG522	B Fly	Tegel
5 Apr 49	Hastings	TG534	E1	Schleswigland
7 Apr 49	York	MW271	AC	Wunstorf
21 Apr 49	Halton	G-AHZZ	E2	Russian Zone
21 Apr 49	York	MW188	E1	Gutersloh
8 May 49	Dakota	KN590	AC Fly	Gatow
10 May 49	Lancaster	G-AKBD	E1	15 miles S of Schwerin
19 May 49	Hastings	TG510	AC	Schleswigland
4 Jun 49	York	MW264	AC	Wunstorf
12 Jun 49	Halifax	G-ALBZ	E1 Breakdown	Tegel
12 Jun 49	Halifax	G-AKBJ	E1 Breakdown	Tegel
18 Jul 49	Hastings	TG573	B Fly	Schleswigland
30 Jul 49	York*	MW145	E1	Wunstorf
15 Aug 49	York*	MW195	B Fly	Wunstorf
Aug 49	Hastings*	TG611	E2	Tegel

Summary

Category	Number
A Assistance	1
AC	15
AC (Fly)	1
B (Non-Fly)	5
B (Fly)	5
E1	12
E2	7
Total	46

* These aircraft were salvaged by Nos 1 and 2 MRSU.

Appendix Six
Operation 'Vittles': Order of Battle, December 1948

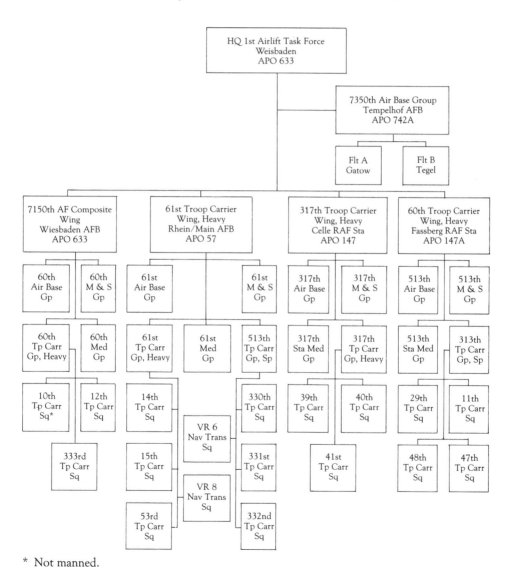

HQ 1st Airlift Task Force Weisbaden APO 633			

7350th Air Base Group Tempelhof AFB APO 742A

Flt A Gatow — Flt B Tegel

7150th AF Composite Wing Wiesbaden AFB APO 633

61st Troop Carrier Wing, Heavy Rhein/Main AFB APO 57

317th Troop Carrier Wing, Heavy Celle RAF Sta APO 147

60th Troop Carrier Wing, Heavy Fassberg RAF Sta APO 147A

60th Air Base Gp — 60th M & S Gp

61st Air Base Gp — 61st M & S Gp

317th Air Base Gp — 317th M & S Gp

513th Air Base Gp — 513th M & S Gp

60th Tp Carr Gp, Heavy — 60th Med Gp

61st Tp Carr Gp, Heavy — 61st Med Gp — 513th Tp Carr Gp, Sp

317th Sta Med Gp — 317th Tp Carr Gp, Heavy

513th Sta Med Gp — 313th Tp Carr Gp, Sp

10th Tp Carr Sq* — 12th Tp Carr Sq

14th Tp Carr Sq — VR 6 Nav Trans Sq — 330th Tp Carr Sq

39th Tp Carr Sq — 40th Tp Carr Sq

29th Tp Carr Sq — 11th Tp Carr Sq

333rd Tp Carr Sq

15th Tp Carr Sq — 331st Tp Carr Sq

41st Tp Carr Sq

48th Tp Carr Sq — 47th Tp Carr Sq

VR 8 Nav Trans Sq

53rd Tp Carr Sq — 332nd Tp Carr Sq

* Not manned.

Glossary

AATO	Army Air Transport Organization
AHQ	Allied Headquarters
AOC	Air Officer Commanding
ARB	Air Registration Board
ATC	Air Traffic Control
BAAS	British American Air Services
BABS	Blind Approach Beacon System
BAFO	British Air Forces of Occupation
BEA	British European Airways
BOAC	British Overseas Airways Corporation
BSAA	British South American Airways
CACC	Civil Aviation Control Commission
CALTF	Combined Airlift Task Force
CDU	Christian Democratic Union
C of A	Certificate of Airworthiness
CRT	Cathode Ray Tube
FASO	Forward Airfield Supply Organization
GCA	Ground Controlled Approach
IAS	Indicated Air Speed
IFR	Instrument Flight Rules
MATS	Military Air Transport Service (US)
MP	Military Police
MRSU	Mobile Repair and Salvage Unit
MT	Mechanical Transport
OEEC	Organization for European Economic Co-operation
PLUTO	Pipeline Under The Ocean

PSP	Pierced Steel Planking
QNH	Part of international 'Q' Code, signifying altimeter setting above sea level

RAAF	Royal Australian Air Force
RAF	Royal Air Force
RASC	Royal Army Service Corps
RASO	Rear Airfield Supply Organization
RIAS	Radio In the American Sector
RNZAF	Royal New Zealand Air Force
R/T	Radio Telephony

SAAF	South African Air Force
SAC	Strategic Air Command (US)
SASO	Senior Air Staff Officer
SDP	Social Democratic Party
SED	Socialist Unity Party (Amalgamated Workers' Party)
SHAFE	Supreme Headquarters Allied Forces Europe

TCG	Troop Carrier Group (US)
TDY	Temporary Duty (US)

UGO	Railway Worker's Union
USAAF	United States Army Air Force (wartime)
USAF	United States Air Force (post-war)
USAFE	United States Air Force, Europe
UV	Undercarriage Visual (Indicators)

VAR	Visual-aural radio range
VFR	Visual Flight Rules
VHF	Very High Frequency

WRAF	Women's Royal Air Force

Index